Ali Ferguson's beautiful, deeply nostalgic textile work takes inspiration from her home and family life, with vintage fabric, hand-embroidered text and found objects combined to create evocative pieces that are imbued with the magic of everyday existence. In this wonderful book Ali reveals the secrets of her work and shares her ingenious methods for finding inspiration at home.

Chapter One explains how to create 'threads of thought' that stem from the tiniest details within the rooms of your home, resulting in extensive mind maps you can use to inspire your finished pieces. Chapter Two shows how to translate these ideas into stitch and select the perfect materials for the mood you want to convey in your work. The rest of the book takes you through the different rooms in a typical home, from kitchen to bedroom, giving a wealth of ideas for finding inspiration from each of these spaces in your own household, accessing memories, stories and emotions to help you create intensely personal and meaningful textile art pieces.

Beautifully illustrated with the author's own work and that of other leading textile artists who draw inspiration from home life, this book revels in cloth and the joy that it brings to every textile artist. It is the ideal book for any artist or embroiderer who wants to explore new sources of inspiration on their very doorstep.

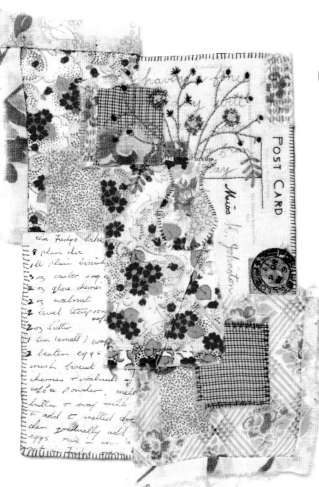

Cloth
Stories

To Iron a Tablecloth

1) Starch in boiling water starch in the proportion of 1-4.
2) Fold a) Pull into shape.
   b) Fold in half right side inside

starch in the proportion of 1-4

Old Bleach
EL.451

15 ins.
No. 3067
EMBROIDERY LINEN
Ivory
An "OLD GLAMIS" Fabric

Cloth Stories

Ali Ferguson

BATSFORD

First published in the United Kingdom
in 2024 by
Batsford
43 Great Ormond Street
London
WC1N 3HZ

An imprint of B. T. Batsford Holdings Limited

ISBN 978 1 84994 818 0

A CIP catalogue record for this book is available from the British Library.

10 9 8 7 6 5 4 3 2

Reproduction by Rival Colour Ltd, UK
Printed and bound by Toppan Leefung Printing Ltd, China

This book can be ordered direct from the publisher at
www.batsfordbooks.com, or try your local bookshop

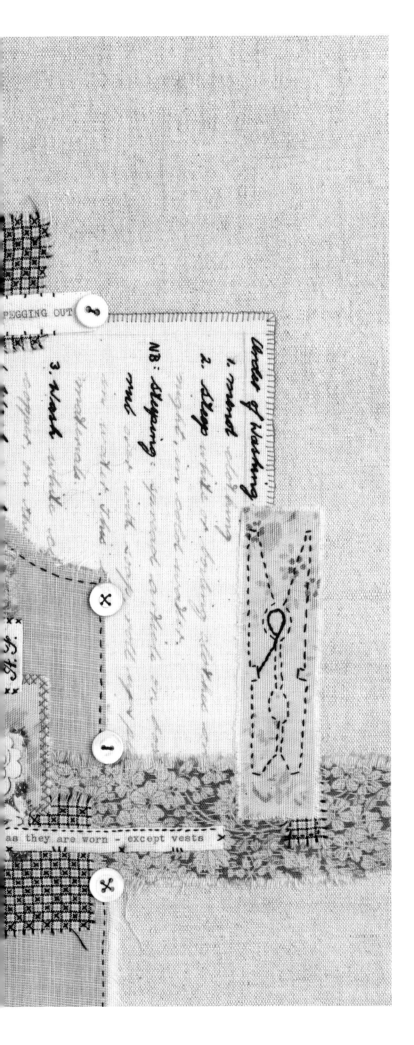

Contents

Introduction

For centuries, cloth has been closely connected to our lives at home. Cosy blankets and quilts that provide warmth, curtains that block out light and cold, clothing that keeps us warm, protects our modesty and expresses our identity, towels that dry, cloths that cover and protect and squares of fabric that wipe away dust, dirt and emotions – the list is endless. Of course, we can't overlook the huge joy that decorative textiles bring to the lives of we cloth lovers as we acknowledge our hunger for creating, collecting and displaying beautiful pieces of cloth embellished with stitch.

This book explores the concept of 'home' and uses it as a theme to create personal textile art. Its aim is to encourage you, the reader, to explore your personal thoughts, stories and emotions of home and to show you how to take these explorations forward into stitching your own cloth stories.

Chapter One looks at creating *threads of thought* – my take on mind mapping. This kick-starts your creative process at the outset of any project. It allows you to dig deeply into a subject, often uncovering the emotions and personal stories that I believe are at the heart of creating meaningful art. I find this a wonderful way of capturing thoughts and ideas on paper. It lies at the heart of my creative practice, and indeed the writing of this book.

Creating personal *threads of thought* is a useful starting point if you wish to work more conceptually, but don't know where to start. Chapter Two addresses this by showing you how to convey personal thoughts into stitch using three simple components: meaningful materials, words and motifs. These aspects are fully explored throughout the book as I take you through the home, room by room. We start in the kitchen, where I share my making process – in this instance, for creating small cloth collages. These are the steps I take when making most of my artwork, adjusting things here and there depending on the materials I am using and the mood I am creating.

From the kitchen we'll move on to the scullery, snug, nursery, and end up in the bedroom, where emotions are exposed and vulnerabilities revealed.

Each chapter starts with suggested *threads of thought*, in the form of a mind map, and this is simply to trigger your own ideas.

My thoughts mostly take me in a nostalgic direction, with memories from childhood and old family ways of life, for example, and this is reflected within my own artwork. However, there are several ideas offered within each mind map that could take you in completely different directions. Believe me, you will find your own. As with any good map, you may find that you are led far away from the subject of *home*.

I strongly recommend that you keep a pen and paper on hand as you read through this book to catch the thoughts and memories that surface before they vanish.

Pages of mind maps on clipboards were at the heart of the planning of this book.

Visual Thinking

I don't know about you, but my thinking doesn't exist in ordered bullet points. Therefore, when I first discovered Tony Buzan's book *How to Mind Map* back in 2002 it resonated with me as a brilliant way to capture my rather scattered thoughts on paper, and I used the process regularly in my work life at the time.

However, it wasn't until six years later, on the first day of my City & Guilds in Experimental Embroidery, when our tutor told us to create a mind map around our chosen theme, that I thought to use this process in my textile work. What a lightbulb moment! It's a process that I've embraced and used ever since.

I love that my thoughts become *visible*. What has previously been a vague notion whirling around inside my head becomes an actual *thing*; something of value that can be explored, organized and remembered.

Over the years, I've gradually developed the mind-mapping process into a personal way of working that I now call creating *threads of thought*.

Why capture your thoughts?

The most immediate answer to this question is to remember them. I'm a thinker; I have lots of random thoughts and ideas popping into my head, and as daily life seems to fill my brain's storage capacity, I need to write things down to remember them.

But there's much more to it than that.

I find that creating *threads of thought* allows one thought to lead easily to another. This takes me in unexpected directions, enabling me to explore a subject from many different angles. If I'm willing to take a bit of time, it will lead me far beyond the obvious ideas, and in so doing often uncovers an underlying emotion. For me, this is the essential part for an interesting and absorbing project: I need to feel an emotional connection to it.

To illustrate what I mean, let's take the theme of 'home' and use 'the kitchen' as an example.

One approach would be to think about kitchen-related items. I love old china and beautiful teapots, and my life often revolves around the kettle and the next cup of tea. I could therefore decide to stitch a little kitchen piece featuring a teacup and saucer; perhaps a plate with a slice of cake or a biscuit. This would make a pleasing combination that would work well in appliqué and stitch. I can pretty much picture the end result, and it would look rather lovely.

But what would happen if I ignored this first inspiration in favour of exploring further, digging deeper and setting off on a journey for which I have no idea what the end result will be?

Exploring the *threads of thought* around my kitchen table soon starts to reveal forgotten stories and emotions.

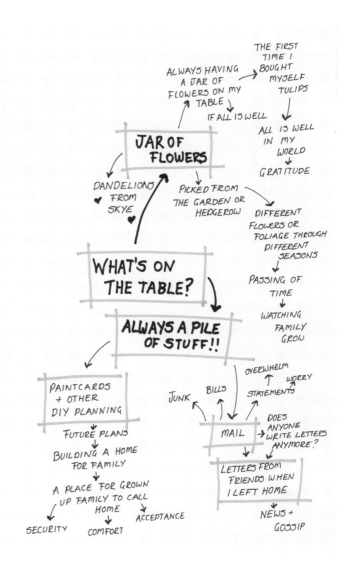

To create my *threads of thought*, I'd cast my eye around my kitchen and jot down what I see. To me, this is the equivalent of making quick preliminary sketches. For example, currently on my kitchen table is a jar of cutlery, a vase of flowers and a messy pile of letters and papers.

There's always a pile of envelopes and mail on my table – which, incidentally, drives me mad. It's mainly bills and junk these days, but I remember when I first left home to start textile college. Aged seventeen, I kept up to date with all the gossip from my friends by writing and receiving letters. There was always a great sense of anticipation when these arrived on my desk in my flat.

Immediately, I have one, or maybe even two, *threads of thought* to follow.

I love having a bunch of flowers on my table. Now these mainly come from my garden, but I can't help thinking about when I was newly married with our first baby at the age of twenty-three. My ex-husband and I were very hard up. I used to go around the supermarket mentally adding up the cost of every item as I put it in my basket. If I bought crisps, I couldn't buy chocolate biscuits, and if I had to buy washing powder then I couldn't buy any biscuits or treats at all. But one day, several years on, I threw a bunch of tulips into the basket. I actually spent a couple of pounds on flowers – a luxury at the time. We'd made it through the very worst of times financially, marking a significant period in my family life. I remember this story simply by looking at a vase of flowers. To this day, when there are flowers on my table, I have a huge sense of wellbeing. There's so much personal emotion around that *thread of thought*.

ABOVE: Hand-stitching on a vintage postcard. Your *threads of thought* can inspire you to be adventurous in your choice of materials.

LEFT: Paint sample cards always remind me of planning our future and creating a family home.

However, I can take it further. Thinking back to this time, when we were struggling and counting every penny, makes me think about the many families currently living below the poverty line within the UK and around the world, and the huge increase in dependence on food banks. By following my *threads of thought*, I've found myself thinking socially and politically. This could take me in several completely different directions, far from my original cosy domestic thoughts. This provides me with many strands of inspiration that I may, or may not, choose to pursue.

I could keep going with an endless stream of stories as I allow my thoughts to wander. A glance at the fridge takes me once more to food, and not only the sense of appreciation of having enough, but also to growing, sourcing, allotments versus air miles, countries of origin, animal welfare, favourite recipes, different cultures, family traditions. I could carry on, and I've not even left the vegetable drawer!

You'll find that by working on your own *threads of thought* you'll access memories, stories and emotions that lead you through each stage of making. If you find the curiosity and willingness to take time to see where your initial idea takes you, you'll create art that is personal and heartfelt. For me, this is deeply satisfying.

Cost of Living, **30 × 30cm (12 × 12in).** Using materials to tell a story. While some dress the table with crisp linen napkins, others struggle to put food on it.

Tools and materials

Paper

I like every part of my making process to be stimulating, so my choice of paper is important to me. I gravitate towards old and discarded paper, and have a particular love of brown parcel paper cut or torn into manageable-sized sheets. I clip these together on a clipboard for working.

Finished pages can be glued, taped or stitched into a sketchbook to organize them, or machine-stitched together into a makeshift book.

Of course, you can work straight into a sketchbook if you wish, or use pristine white or coloured paper – whatever sets your heart fluttering.

For many years I created my *threads of thought* on the backs of used envelopes. I found that if I worked straight into a sketchbook page, I could easily get side-tracked. I fretted that my writing wasn't 'pretty' enough, or that my layout wasn't 'arty' enough, and I'd find myself editing my thoughts before capturing them on paper. This didn't happen with an old envelope.

But use whatever works for you – some people draw their mind maps on their tablet or computer.

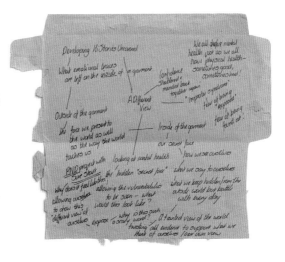

Pens

I like to have two or three colours of pen, including a highlighter in a colour that will stand out from my main writing.

Additional items

Additional pieces of scrap paper or luggage labels are useful for adding notes. I collect offcuts from other projects – lined papers, vellum, graph paper – and keep these to hand in a tin. I like to use these to add extra information and notes, particularly if I am collating everything into a sketchbook.

ABOVE: *Threads of thought* jotted down on an old envelope went on to inspire *Not Just Blue* on page 120.

BELOW: Gather pens and papers that you love using to create your own *threads of thought*.

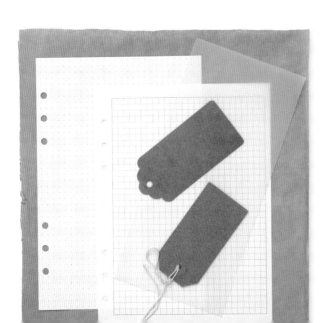

Getting Started

The process of mind mapping or creating *threads of thought* is simple. Try not to overthink or censor your thoughts, and write quickly without steering them in any particular direction. The key is to allow words to flow until they feel forced, and then stop.

Let's start our journey around the house by going back to the kitchen: the hub of the household for many.

- Start by writing the word 'kitchen' in the centre of your page. Take yourself to your kitchen, or imagine yourself there looking around.

- Quickly jot down the things that immediately catch your eye until you have five or six headings – perhaps items like table, fridge, sink, washing machine, cooker and shelves. Write all around your central title, leaving space in between. Each time you write something, draw a line from the word *kitchen* to connect it.

- Next, look at everything you have written and choose one title that attracts your attention. Highlight it in some way, perhaps with a different-coloured pen.

- Now start writing down your thoughts. Relax and allow one to lead to another, jotting down everything, however random, and making connecting lines between.

- *Cooker* could take me to cooking, baking, favourite recipes and the people I associate with them. Before I know it, memories and emotions start to flood in.

- Often you find when writing a few words that there's a whole story behind them. Don't try to write lots of details, just enough to trigger your memories.

- When your thoughts start to slow, move onto another title and repeat the process. You might find yourself jumping around from one to another; this is perfectly okay. The beauty of this process is that it 'captures' your thoughts just as they occur.

- Keep going for as long as the thoughts flow. You might need to use some additional scraps of paper if you run out of space under one title – I simply tape or pin these to my original page. I always end up with something that looks quite scrappy, but yours may end up neat and methodical, depending on your way of working.

- One of your titles may become a whole new *thread of thought* in itself. Simply take a new page of paper, write your title in the centre and take it from there.

- Don't panic if you find this difficult; I begin each chapter with some *threads of thought* to get you started.

If you are still struggling, don't try to force the process, but have a notebook or some scraps of paper to hand and jot things down whenever they occur to you. Your own memories and ideas will be stimulated by reading some of my stories throughout this book. Often if you relax and turn your attention elsewhere, things will come to mind spontaneously. Capture them by writing them down.

I write my personal *threads of thought* on brown parcel paper – so much less intimidating than a pristine white page. Your *threads of thought* may take more than one page. If so, allow them to spill out onto extra pages.

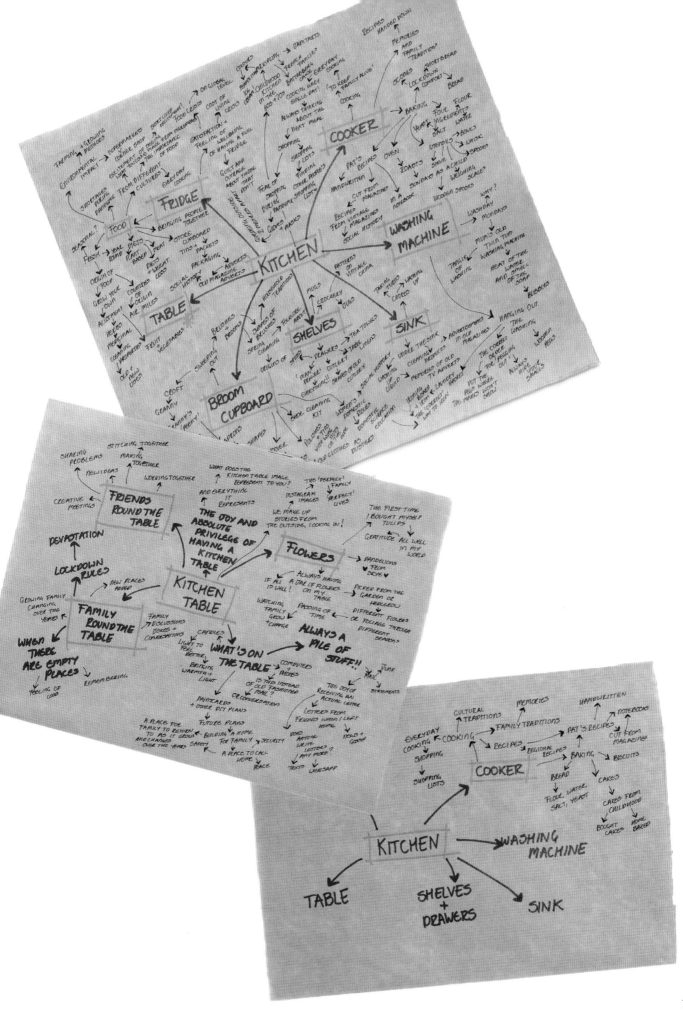

15

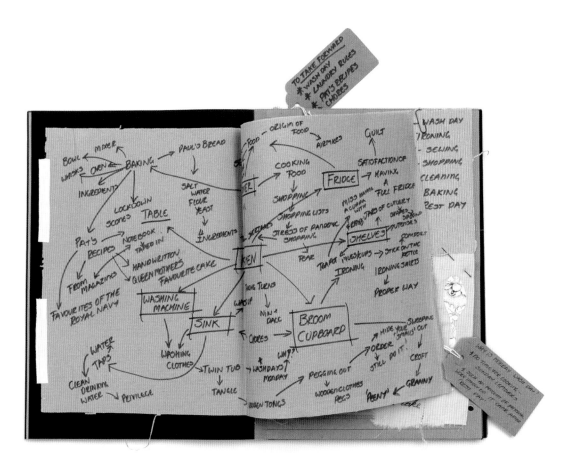

Gathering your thoughts

At this point, you've probably gathered an almost overwhelming amount of information that you can't possibly incorporate all into one piece of work. One thread of thought could inspire many textile projects for years to come.

- Step back from your page and cast your eye over it as a whole. Mark or highlight the things that particularly attract your attention. These could be things that make you smile, create a sense of comfort, nostalgia or familiarity. Perhaps it's something that interests you, that you'd like to find out more about. Equally, they could be things that make you angry or frustrate you. The thoughts that provoke an emotional response within you are the ones that are of interest; that's when you know your story is personal and worth pursuing.

- If your *threads of thought* threw up a question or a subject that you would like to know more about, jot down your findings on another piece of paper. Perhaps you'll be inspired to embark on extensive research about that subject.

- Having identified the areas that pique your interest, take note of them on a separate piece of paper. In so doing, you've gathered together a personally stimulating collection of thoughts and ideas to take forward into a piece, or a series, of textile work.

Let's now return to my question of *why capture your thoughts?* Will it actually make any difference to your end results?

In Chapter Two you will look at using *threads of thought* as a way to inspire your choice of materials. Perhaps you will find yourself using materials that you wouldn't previously have thought of; things that add a deeper layer of interest to your work and make people curious. Why is the decoration on a floral teacup made from a newspaper article about food banks? Why is that kitchen 'still life' stitched on an old envelope?

Perhaps you will include words from favourite family recipes, or from remembered conversations that took place around the table. These words may have no meaning to anyone else but you.

I love other artists' work that causes me to wonder. But not everything is visible. I agree that no one looking at a vase of flowers on one of my cloth collages will know the story behind it unless I tell them, but that doesn't mean the story isn't there. As I write down each *thread of thought*, I bring these memories alive and I then weave them into my work stitch by stitch.

I passionately believe that it is the hidden presence of your stories and memories that brings an energy and vibrancy to your textile work, and it is the unseen presence of these that others find themselves inexplicably connecting to. Something in your work awakens a story within them. Why else would we find our hearts stirring when looking at pieces of cloth stitched together by a complete stranger?

OPPOSITE:
Sketchbook page – I'm starting to gather my thoughts by highlighting the ideas I wish to explore further.

BELOW: *Port Elizabeth* (detail). Even if you can't see the story behind my vase of flowers, that doesn't mean it isn't there.

Turning Thoughts into Stitch

So now you have your *threads of thought* captured on paper and have extracted some interesting ideas that you would like to take further. If you've worked in this way before, you may be buzzing with ideas for how you could take these into stitching using your own unique toolkit of techniques. However, if this is new to you, this next stage might feel daunting.

You have all these thoughts, but where do you go from here? How do you begin to translate your stories and emotions into stitch?

Here are three simple elements to use as starting points:

- Meaningful materials
- Words
- Motifs

We will discuss these elements in detail on the following pages.

Meaningful materials

By 'meaningful', I mean materials that are relevant to your ideas and will contribute to your storytelling. Rather than going with what is immediately obvious, start by writing your *threads of thought*. For example, if you continue with the kitchen theme, write 'kitchen materials' in the centre of your page and start writing in the same way as before. If your previous mind maps have taken you in a different direction, then write a relevant title.

Fabrics

My immediate thoughts take me to kitchen fabrics such as tea towels and table linen. However, as I write my *threads of thought* I remember the jumble of washing coming out of my mum's twin tub: shirts wound around bed sheets, collars, cuffs and button bands all tangled as one and, rather randomly, a brown polka-dot summer dress! I remember my granny's apron – or 'peeny', as we always called it – damask tablecloths with blue stripes around the edges and my mum's hand-embroidered tray cloths immaculately stitched on crisp linen with the designs printed in blue ink. As soon as I start thinking along these lines, my emotions become involved. I have memories of my mum sitting on the doorstep stitching as she watched over us playing on the street outside.

My senses also become engaged. I can smell the hot soapy bubbles of the washing machine, feel my dress against

BELOW AND OPPOSITE: A collection of 'meaningful materials' inspired by my kitchen *threads of thought*. If you explore your memories in this way you will come up with an interesting and evocative collection of materials to work with.

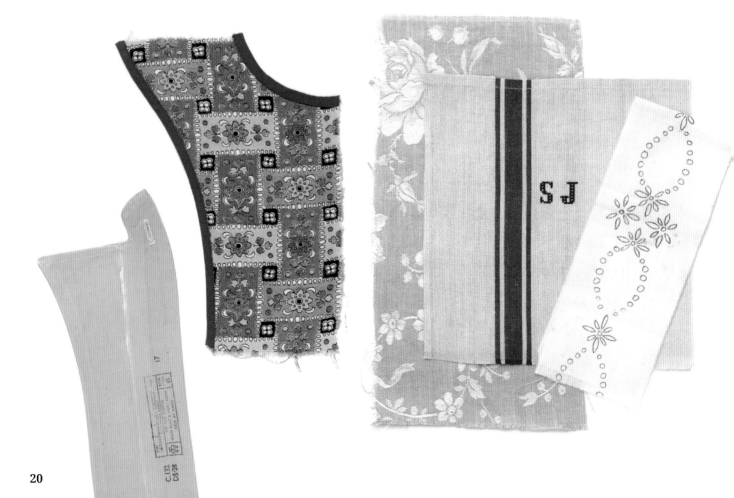

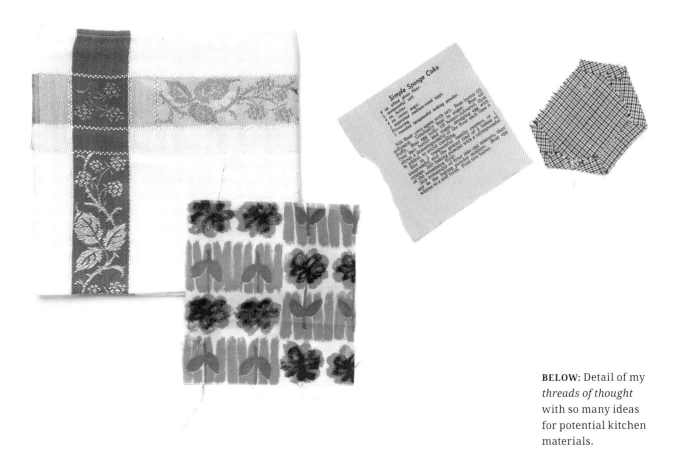

my bare legs and hear the words of my gran, in her peeny, leaning on the fence issuing dire warnings of what would happen if we left the gate open (her aged dog, who never left the fireside, would take to the hills and never be seen again).

If I choose fabrics that connect me to these memories, then I am already emotionally invested in my storytelling. Sadly, I will never have a piece of fabric from my granny's peeny, but often when I see 1940s cotton prints, they transport me to her wrap-over aprons and my most vivid memories of her.

Paper

You may wish to include 'paper' as one of the headings in your *threads of thought*. As well as food packaging or labels, your 'kitchen papers' could include pages from recipe books, handwritten recipes and kitchen-related pages from magazines.

Can I stitch it?

What about other materials that could help you tell your story? How inventive can you be in finding ways to add stitch? Consider any relevant material and ask yourself 'Can I stitch it?' – or perhaps, even better, 'How can I stitch it?'

A stitch is made by pulling a threaded needle in and out of your material, so what kitchen materials or objects already have holes in them? How could you use these holes to create stitches?

If the composition of the material does not allow the needle to pass through it easily, perhaps you could create holes. Open your mind to different things in this way and experiment.

Let's Bake,
**17 × 30cm
(6¾ × 12in).** Words
stitched using soft
embroidery thread
onto an old kitchen
sieve using lettering
from an old cross
stitch chart.

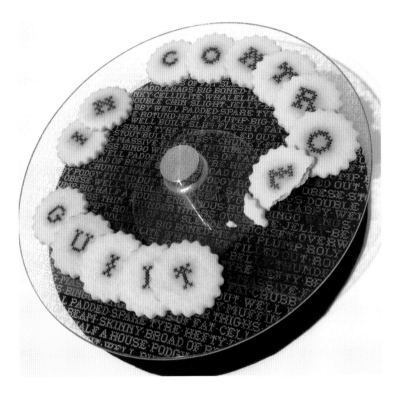

ABOVE: Caren Garfen, *Guilt Biscuits*, 30 × 30 × 8cm (12 × 12 × 3in). Butter biscuits stitched with silk threads on a laser-cut glass platter.

ABOVE RIGHT: Vanessa Marr, *You Shall Go to the Ball*, 5 × 20cm (2 × 8in). Hand-embroidered rubber gloves. Vanessa's choice of material has immediate impact in her storytelling.

In her piece *Guilt Biscuits*, artist Caren Garfen laser-cut holes in butter biscuits to enable her to stitch the words 'guilt' and 'in control' through them. These words were specifically chosen as they represent two of the many issues facing those dealing with anorexia nervosa and bulimia. They sit on a glass platter that has been laser-cut with words that echo through the minds of people with eating disorders.

Artist Vanessa Marr embroidered ordinary household rubber gloves in her piece *You Shall Go to the Ball*.

Her inspired use of materials is a fundamental part of her storytelling.

If you choose your materials in this way, you place them at the very heart of your cloth stories and they will be a reflection of your own memories, areas of interest, emotions, culture and experiences. I'll give suggestions for meaningful materials at the start of each chapter to help trigger your own ideas, but if you create your own *threads of thought* you'll come up with many more of your own.

Words

I have a passion for words, even
though I find conversation in most
social settings pretty terrifying.
I include words in some form in most
of my textile pieces. I'm particularly
fascinated by other people's words.
I love reading old letters and postcards
written by complete strangers and
poring over old magazines with their
documentation of everyday life of that
time. Sentences will jump out at me as
I read these, but it also happens when
I am listening to interviews, podcasts
or the news on the radio. Whenever
this happens, I write down the
words on scrap paper and keep them
somewhere safe to remember them.
I call this 'thought catching'. Captured
in a sketchbook, these can be used as
prompts or bursts of inspiration for
future projects.

Handwriting

I especially love handwritten words.
Handwriting is a form of personal
mark-making, much like stitching.
Handwriting can be beautiful in itself,
especially that found on old paper
ephemera where the letters have been
crafted with a pen and ink. But even
more than that, I think of it as a physical
representation of the thoughts and
feelings of the writer at that point in
time and that handwritten words have
the ability to capture the emotion at the
exact moment of pen hitting paper.

OPPOSITE AND BELOW: Look out for vintage ephemera with handwritten text. I especially love finding little notes on the back of old envelopes – mundane moments captured forever.

BELOW RIGHT: *Marmalade, Butter and Jam* (detail). I traced words from a found shopping list and then hand-stitched them onto this collage.

Where to find words and text

Anywhere and everywhere! Create another page of *threads of thought* to explore where you might find words that will add to your story. If you take time to do this, you'll be surprised at what long-forgotten memories drop into your head.

You can add a personal element to your work by using words from your memories, thoughts and feelings on a theme. You could use words and phrases that you associate with a family member or a loved one, a remembered conversation, words that children mispronounced or misspelt.

Start noticing words from handwritten recipes, diaries, school jotters, letters, postcards, ledgers or documents, or you could quote facts and figures that you have found during research. Don't forget about the huge resource of email, social media platforms and text messages.

I love finding words in random places, notes scribbled in the margins of a book or an old knitting pattern, words that someone else has underlined or highlighted, or a shopping list on the back of an old envelope.

Note: Be aware of copyright issues connected to the use of other people's words. I avoid using any material where copyright is an issue.

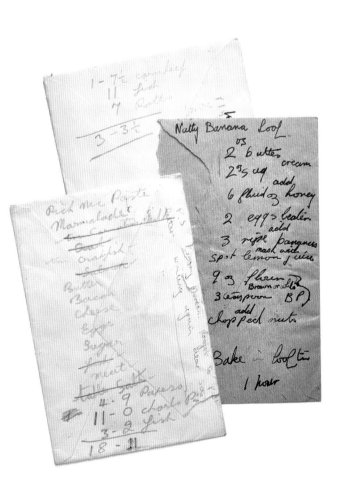

Hand-stitching words

This is my favourite way of creating handwritten text on fabric. It is a slow process, but I love that I give real value to the words by the amount of time that I am willing to invest in stitching them.

- If you are using words from old paper ephemera – a letter, for example – make a photocopy so that you don't damage the original with handling. You can also enlarge or reduce the size of the text at this stage.

- Trace the words that you are using onto tracing paper or vellum using a dark, fine-nibbed pen. You can alter the layout to fit your space.

- Words are read easily if they are stitched onto a lightweight, light-coloured fabric. This also allows you to trace them directly onto your fabric. Use masking tape to attach your tracing paper onto a lightbox if you have one and tape your fabric on top. If you don't have a lightbox, you can tape your fabric and vellum to a window.

- Use a sharp pencil and a light touch. Hold the fabric taut as you are working and draw your lines just dark enough to see when stitching. The pencil line will be covered by the solid line of stitching. You could use an erasable fabric pen if you prefer, but I like a fine pencil line.

- Attach the fabric to your collage background before stitching, unless it is very thick.

- I use a backstitch (this covers the pencil line) and either one strand of stranded cotton or a fine sewing thread (the type you would use in a sewing machine). If you are working to a bigger scale, you may wish to use a thicker thread or a different stitch.

- Look for stitching inspiration: cross-stitch charts, old samplers or transfers for stitching monograms.

Typewriters and tape

I love the look of typewriter text and often type onto tape or ribbon. I do this by putting a piece of double-sided tape across a piece of paper, loading the paper into my typewriter, peeling off the paper strip and sticking my fabric tape along the bottom edge. Adjust your typewriter so that it will type across the middle of your tape.

BELOW: Sample showing the various stages I use when hand stitching words.

OPPOSITE: *Port Elizabeth*, 25 × **34cm (10 × 13½in).** Cloth collage with text from vintage magazine papers, handstitched words and phrases from an old recipe book typed onto tape.

planned to meet the needs of a busy housewife

KOOP
UNIE LENING
SERTIFIKATE

PORT ELIZABETH
DEC 12
1923

UNION LOAN
CERTIFICATE

Bake it With Royal and be Sure

satisfy the appetite of your family

Chocolate Filling and Icing
whites of 2 eggs
2 cups confectioner's sugar
2½ tablespoons milk
1 teaspoon vanilla extract
4 ounces unsweetened chocolate
1 teaspoon butter

Beat whites until stiff; add sugar slowly, beating well; add milk, vanilla and
chocolate which has been melted with
butter; mix until smooth. Spread on cake.

Old-Fashioned Chocolate Filling
3 ounces unsweetened chocolate
3 tablespoons milk
1 egg
½ cup powder

beat with beater for seven minutes. Add ½
teaspoon flavoring and baking powder; beat and spread on cake.
For "Chocolate Icing" add to above 1½
ounces melted unsweetened chocolate 2
minutes before taking from fire.
For "Coffee Icing" add 3 tablespoons
cold boiled coffee in place of water.

Raisin Drop Cakes
4 tablespoons shortening
1 cup sugar
1 egg
⅔ cup milk
1⅔ cups flour
3 teaspoons Royal Baking Powder
¼ teaspoon salt
1 cup raisins
1 teaspoon vanilla extract

Cream shortening; add sugar;
beaten egg and milk very slowly;
flour, baking powder and salt which
been sifted together; add raisins w
have been washed, drained and flo
slightly; add flavoring, mix well. P
small amount of mixture into
greased individual cake tin and bak
hot oven 15 to 20 minutes. Sprinkle
powdered sugar, or cover with icing

Orange Ca
4 tablespoons
1 cup sugar
¾ cup milk
1 egg
2 cups flour
3 teaspoons
¾ teaspoon
1 teaspoon o
grated rind o

Macaroons
2 small
4 oz
4 oz
1 oz

and earn the compliments from your friends

20-25
180°

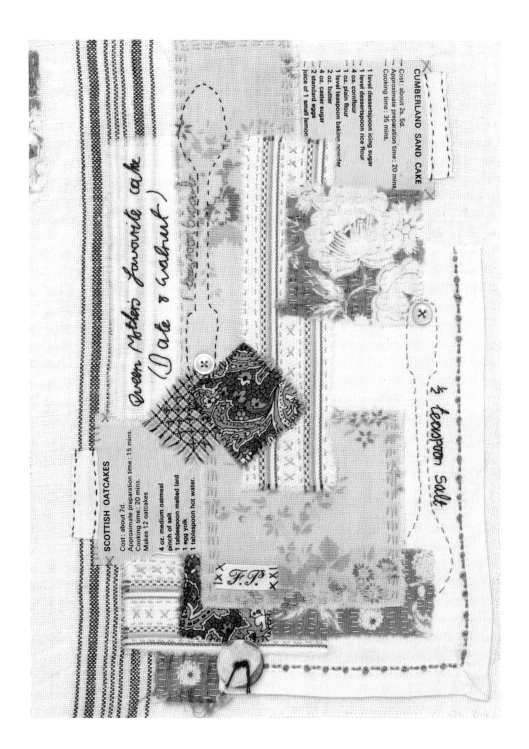

Motifs

By motifs I mean something you can use to help illustrate your story. Start off by thinking of simple line drawings that you could create in stitch. For example, for the kitchen it could be a piece of cutlery, weighing scales, a piece of fruit or a vegetable, a bag of flour or a mixing bowl. Equally, I might choose to use a vase of flowers, an envelope or a postcard, as these motifs relate meaningfully to my personal kitchen memories. Create more *threads of thought* to help you come up with ideas.

A lovely way to create a motif outline is to do your own simple line drawing. Don't be put off if you don't feel confident at drawing: there are many ways to create a simple motif outline.

Line drawing motifs

- Create a 'still life' and take a photograph of it. Print your image onto paper and trace it.

- If you have your own home copier you can photocopy objects, enabling you to trace the outlines.

- Sometimes you can draw around the object.

- Search online for 'line drawing of a teapot', for example. Many images in a huge variety of styles will come up. Looking at these simplified versions might just give you the confidence you need to create your own.

- You could always ask a friend to do some drawings for you. It is meaningful to include another person's energy and story into your work!

- You can also play around with size and scale of your drawings by photocopying.

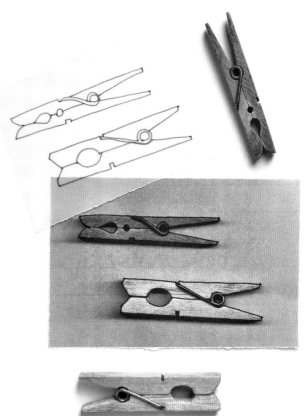

LEFT: Sample showing stages of stitching a simple teaspoon motif. I often use masking tape to hold the paper in place.

OPPOSITE: When using patterned fabric, I carefully consider the placement of my outline before ironing down the Bondaweb. I've added small areas of buttonhole stitching along the edges of the stitched samples.

Hand-stitched motifs

You'll see that many of my cloth collages have a motif outline stitched in either a running stitch or a backstitch – though it isn't actually a backstitch!. To do this:

- Trace your outline onto white tissue paper. It's important that the paper can tear easily.

- Pin or tape the tissue paper in place and stitch with a running stitch over the pencil lines through the tissue paper. Hold it taut as you work and make small, regular stitches, keeping a firm tension.

- Once you have completed your stitched outlines, carefully tear away the tissue paper: hold your thumb over the stitches as you tear to protect them from pulling. It can be helpful to use tweezers to get rid of the last tiny bits of tissue.

- If I want a solid line (that looks like a backstitch), I work another line of stitches, filling in the gaps.

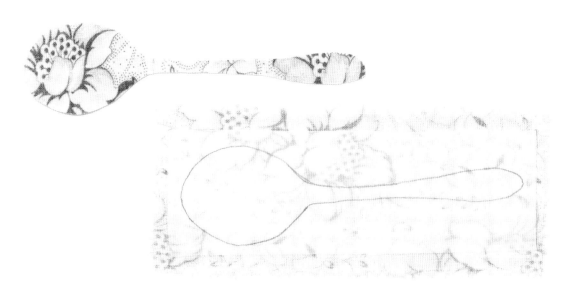

Appliquéd motifs

A quick and effective way to create simple appliquéd motifs is to use a fusible web. This is a web of adhesive that comes with a paper backing and can be used to bond two layers of fabric together when heat is applied with an iron. I use the brand Bondaweb.

- Depending on your motif, you may need to reverse the image before starting.

- Draw your motif on the paper side of the Bondaweb and cut out, leaving a small border all around.

- Place the rough side of the Bondaweb onto the wrong side of your fabric and iron until stuck. I always cover my work with a piece of baking parchment when using Bondaweb to protect it (and the iron) from glue mishaps.

- Carefully cut out along the line of your motif and peel off the backing paper.

- Position the motif onto your work, fabric side up, and iron.

- Stitch along the edges.

Gathering materials together

For me, the key to creating art with 'story' at its heart is to gather together my materials, words and motifs while my head is still immersed in my *threads of thought*, while my memories are fresh and the emotion is real. Don't be tempted to rush this part: it's an essential part of the making process.

At this point I don't worry too much about colours. I simply go to my stash and gather the fabrics that speak to me. If I start gathering while my thoughts are still full of stories and memories, then I know that there will be an emotional connection with anything I am choosing. If I want to include papers, I'll also search through my old magazines and set aside anything of interest.

Personally, my love and fascination is for vintage materials, used, washed and worn, and I tend to only use natural fabrics, mainly cotton and linen. I love old

garments, blankets, sheeting, quilts – pretty much anything homely, but your gathering will relate to your own *threads of thought* and may be very different to mine.

On a practical note, I don't usually use a frame or hoop when I am making my cloth collages. For these, I always need to consider what fabric I am going to use as a foundation. It needs to be something that is easy to stitch through but has a bit of body to it. I love using vintage table linen, tea towels and old woollen blankets.

BELOW: I love using 'homely' fabrics – scraps of blanket, quilts and table linens especially those with beautiful edgings.

OPPOSITE: Old needlework samples pinned into a sketchbook are a valuable source for stitching inspiration.

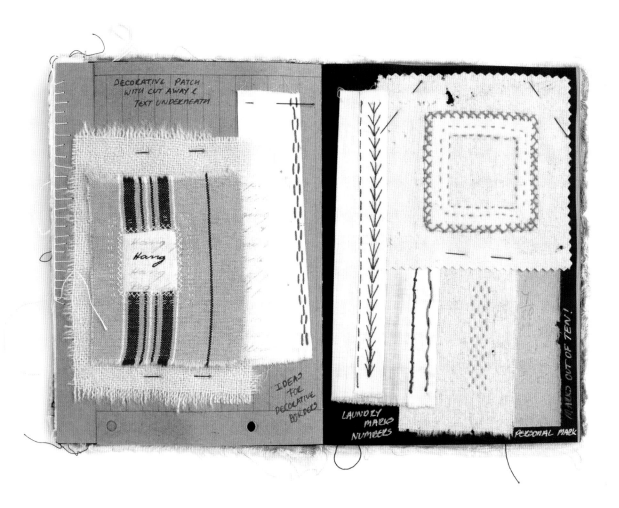

Inside the image (handwritten notes):
DECORATIVE PATCH WITH CUT AWAY & TEXT UNDERNEATH

Hang

IDEAS FOR DECORATIVE BORDERS

LAUNDRY MARKS NUMBERS

PERSONAL MARK

Inspiration for hand-stitching

I describe myself as a 'stitcher' rather than an embroiderer. I don't create perfectly formed embroidery stitches and I've never learned the 'correct' way to do things, but I have always stitched.

As a child, my home was filled with fabrics, with a great big 'rag bag' full of scraps that we turned to whenever my dolls needed a new outfit. We had canvas for needlework, tea cloths with blue transfers, every kind of thread, and pretty much everything we could possibly need to make, mend, patch or decorate any textile surface.

I find vintage school samples and textbooks to be a lovely source of inspiration. I'm always awed by the exquisite stitching made by young girls from the days when training in needlework was an essential part of girls' education.

From what I can remember, my own school learning consisted mainly of cross stitches on various sizes of canvas. It was not hugely adventurous, but I still find it hard to resist stitching a cross into each square of a gingham scrap.

You could find it valuable to create your own *threads of thought* around the theme of sewing to see what memories and personal stories this will unlock, bringing your own history, however distant or recent, into each stitched mark you make.

My favourite stitches

I tend to work with a very few favourite stitches – a small collection of personal marks that I use repeatedly across my body of work. They are mainly straight stitches: running stitch, backstitch, cross stitch, seeding and herringbone. I also love blanket stitch as an edging.

I use these stitches to create pattern combinations that I work down the sides and across the edges of fabric patches in my cloth collages.

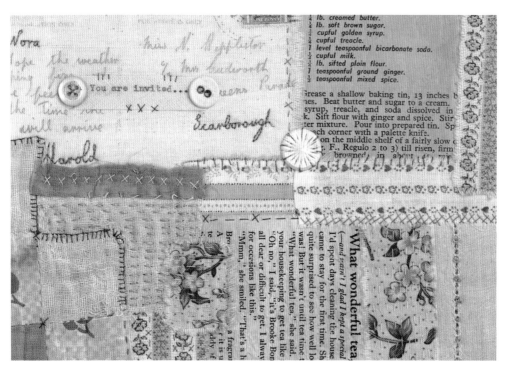

ABOVE: Sample showing ideas for decorative stitching – the simplest of stitches and stitch patterns are often the most effective.

LEFT: *Dear Nora,* **(detail).** Detail of cloth collage showing some of different stitches that I use repeatedly in my work.

A word about threads

I prefer to select threads from my stash for each new piece of work rather than buying specifically, but of course this only works because I have a good selection to choose from. I encourage you to buy threads as and when they catch your eye in order to build up your personal collection.

I love to use vintage threads, sewing threads on old wooden reels, embroidery silks and mending cottons, but this is personal preference and it does come with some problems. Sometimes the thread has deteriorated and breaks easily, and of course a thread can seldom be repeated once it runs out. On the plus side, as well as the satisfaction of using a thread from someone else's collection, it does often mean that when I am choosing from what I have, I come up with colour combinations that I might not have chosen if I were buying new.

Probably the most useful thread to collect is stranded embroidery cottons, which are available in every shade of every colour. You can vary the number of strands that you use depending on how thick you want the thread to be. I work with a fine thread, either one or two strands, or sewing cottons (like you would use on a sewing machine). Take time to experiment by creating stitch samples in different threads and you'll soon find favourites that you will return to over and over.

Kitchen Stories

My first kitchen *threads of thought* unearthed so many ideas that I split it into two chapters! The pieces that I have created for this chapter are inspired by my kitchen table, my thoughts around food and cooking and, more specifically, my late mother-in-law and her recipes. These ideas have so many memories and emotions attached to them that I could keep stitching their stories for years to come.

Kitchen Threads of Thought

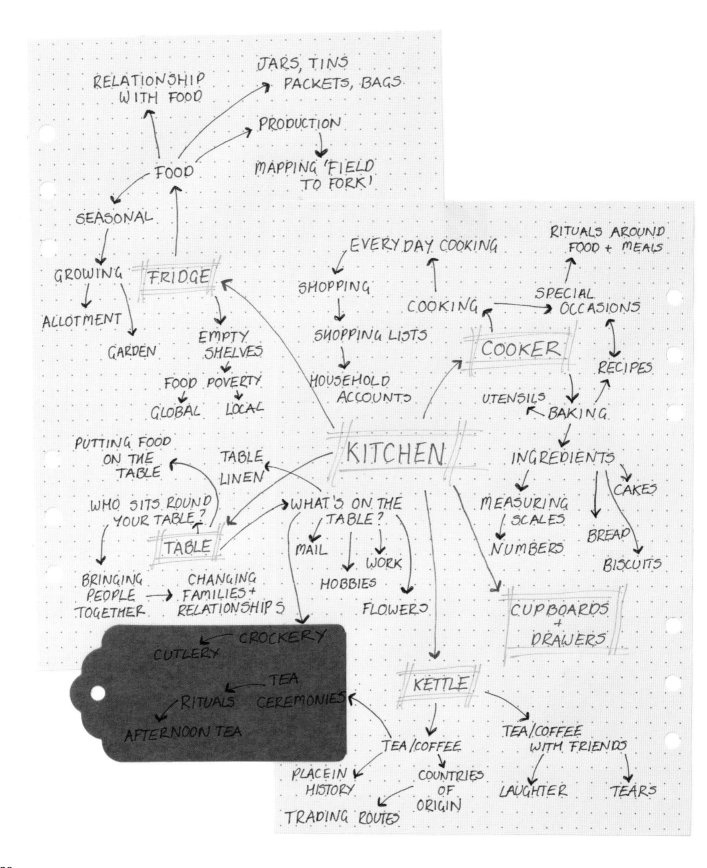

RELATIONSHIP WITH FOOD

JARS, TINS PACKETS, BAGS

PRODUCTION

MAPPING 'FIELD TO FORK'

FOOD

SEASONAL

GROWING

ALLOTMENT

GARDEN

FRIDGE

EMPTY SHELVES

FOOD POVERTY

GLOBAL   LOCAL

EVERY DAY COOKING

SHOPPING

SHOPPING LISTS

HOUSEHOLD ACCOUNTS

COOKING

RITUALS AROUND FOOD + MEALS

SPECIAL OCCASIONS

COOKER

RECIPES

UTENSILS   BAKING

INGREDIENTS

KITCHEN

PUTTING FOOD ON THE TABLE

TABLE LINEN

WHO SITS ROUND YOUR TABLE?

TABLE

WHAT'S ON THE TABLE?

MAIL   WORK

HOBBIES

FLOWERS

MEASURING SCALES

NUMBERS

CAKES

BREAD

BISCUITS

BRINGING PEOPLE TOGETHER

CHANGING FAMILIES + RELATIONSHIPS

CUPBOARDS + DRAWERS

CROCKERY

CUTLERY

TEA

RITUALS   CEREMONIES

AFTERNOON TEA

KETTLE

TEA/COFFEE

PLACE IN HISTORY

COUNTRIES OF ORIGIN

TRADING ROUTES

TEA/COFFEE WITH FRIENDS

LAUGHTER   TEARS

CHECKS, FLORALS

POLKA DOTS, STRIPES

DAMASK TABLECLOTHS

EMBROIDERED TABLE LINENS

NAPKINS WITH INITIALS

VINTAGE FRENCH TEA TOWELS

OLD GRAIN SACK COTTONS

KITCHEN DYED COTTONS

USING ONION SKINS, BEETROOT,

TEA, COFFEE ETC.

PAPERS:

   SHOPPING LISTS

   RECEIPTS

   PACKAGING

   HANDWRITTEN RECIPES

   ADVERTS + RECIPES SNIPPED

   FROM OLD MAGAZINES

X Words X

PERSONAL RECOLLECTIONS

REMEMBERED CONVERSATIONS

PERSONAL PHRASES

HANDWRITTEN RECIPES

OLD MAGAZINE ARTICLES + ADVERTS

WORDS OF WISDOM FROM OLD COOKERY BOOKS

FOOD PACKAGING + LABELS

INGREDIENTS

SHOPPING LISTS

RECEIPTS

QUANTITIES + NUMBERS

BAKING OR COOKING WORDS: WHISK, FOLD, BEAT

DATA FROM RESEARCH

X Motifs X

JAM JARS, BOTTLES, PACKETS & BAGS

CUTLERY

TEA / COFFEE POTS, CUPS, SAUCERS & PLATES

PATTERNS FOUND ON OLD CHINA

CAKE STANDS, BISCUITS & CAKES

MIXING BOWLS, ROLLING PINS & WHISKS

FRUIT & VEGETABLES

PATTERNS FROM EMBROIDERED TABLE LINEN

VASES & JARS OF FLOWERS

RECIPE

Mixture
1 lb. Spillers
Self-Raising Flour
10 oz. margarine
10 oz. caster su
5 eggs
½ lb. sultan
6 oz. glacé c
2 oz. angeli
2 oz. mixe
2 oz. whol
1 oz. grou
grated ri

Marshm
8 level t
icing s
1 lb. gr
2 egg
½ cup w

Pat's recipes

My mother-in-law, Pat, lived on her own for most of the time that I knew her, and food didn't play a particularly important role in her later life. Therefore, it came as a surprise once she passed away when I came across a huge bag stuffed full of recipes. These were handwritten on the backs of envelopes, on bits of cardboard and scraps of paper taped into notebooks, as well as recipes carefully snipped out of magazines. They represented a whole life that I had never known, as Pat was well into her sixties when I first met her. Suddenly I had a glimpse of this young woman entertaining in the 1960s and 1970s and the decades of everyday family cooking and baking. I found the bag stuffed down by the side of her

armchair, so this huge collection of recipes was obviously important to her. I can picture her picking up the bag and rummaging through it and, I'm sure, remembering so many people gathered around her own table over the years.

I particularly loved the personal recipes such as 'John Patterson's Nana's Cake' and I loved the sweeping statements of some titles such as 'Queen Mother's Favourite Cake' ('Date & Walnut' added in brackets just in case there was any doubt). My particular favourite is an old Scout recipe of my husband's: 'Hammy, eggy, cheesy topsides – favourite of the Royal Navy'. It makes my heart smile thinking of the mum who kept her boy's recipe for over fifty years in a bag beside her chair.

ABOVE: 'Favourite of the Royal Navy' – stitched words that will forever remind me of my late mother-in-law.

OPPOSITE: Raiding Pat's precious bag of recipes has provided me with an endless and truly meaningful source of words to use in my work.

Creating your own meaningful cloth

I've successfully printed my own 'handwritten' fabrics for years using my home inkjet printer, and they have become a key component in much of my work. It's very satisfying to create your own personal fabrics such as those printed from Pat's precious handwritten recipes.

I only use pieces of handwriting that I personally own to avoid any copyright issues.

Note: the following instructions are for inkjet printers only.

Inkjet-printing

There are so many differences between models of printers that I can only speak from my own experience of printing, but here are my general tips and conclusions:

- Fabric sheets are available that are ready-prepared to go through an inkjet printer, simply by following the instructions on the pack.

- These prepared sheets are expensive, so I tend to prepare my own by using fine, lightweight, cotton fabrics, or sometimes a silk organza. A tightly woven fabric will give a more detailed print than a loose weave. Your fabric can't be too thick or it won't feed through the printer.

- I use freezer paper to stabilize the fabric and allow it to be fed through the printer. I prefer ready-cut sheets rather than a roll.

Printing on fabric

- I use the photocopy facility on my printer, but you can also scan your document into your computer, enhancing it with photo-editing software and print it from there. Make a test copy onto paper first and make any adjustments such as altering the size.

- Cut a piece of fabric slightly larger than your sheet of freezer paper and lay it on an ironing board. Place the shiny surface of the freezer paper face down onto your fabric and iron (dry) until the fabric is stuck, paying particular attention to the edges.

- Carefully trim away the excess fabric. Snip away any stray threads. Iron once again after trimming, checking once more that the edges are firmly stuck down.

- Place in your printer feed tray to ensure that it will print onto the fabric side and print as normal. You may need to experiment to find the best print settings for your printer, but I use standard print settings.

- Peel away the freezer paper backing. This can be used several times over. Iron your print.

I only use this process for wall art that will not be washed. If you leave your fabric untreated then the ink will run/wash out to some degree if it comes in contact with liquid. There are, however, products available, such as C. Jenkins Bubble Jet Set 2000, that will make your prints colourfast to a degree. Fading will occur if it is hung in direct sunlight, but I've not found this to be an issue over the many years that I've used this process.

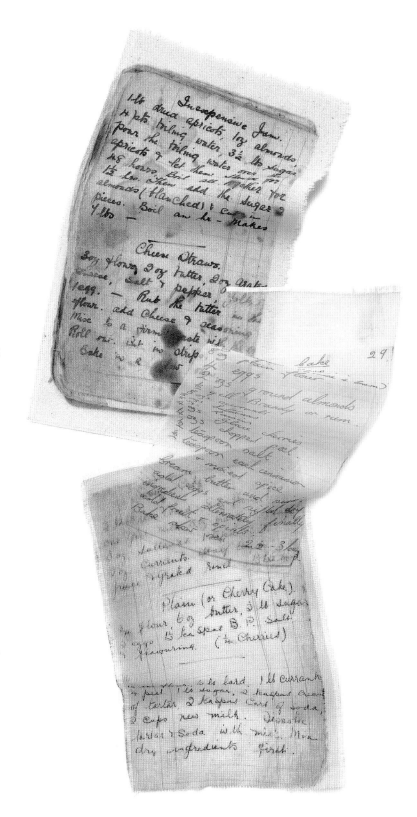

The same recipe printed onto calico (top), silk organza (middle) and muslin (bottom).

Cloth story collage

Returning to our three elements of meaningful materials, words and motifs, we'll now look at using these, along with our *threads of thought*, to create a personal cloth story collage.

Marmalade, Butter and Jam, 26 × 37cm (10¼ × 14½in). Cloth collage inspired by a found shopping list written on the back of an old envelope.

STEP ONE: GATHERING

- Once you've completed your kitchen *threads of thought*, it's time to start collecting materials. At this point you have been so immersed in the thinking behind your kitchen story that you can be very intuitive with this. Have a good rummage through your stash, collecting together the things that you feel drawn to. Don't worry too much about colours; allow yourself to gather and a colour story will emerge later.

- You will need a piece of fabric such as linen or medium-weight cotton to use as your background. In my sample I've used an old French tea towel. Start with a piece approximately 18 × 25cm (7 × 10in) for a small cloth collage.

- Create your inkjet-printed fabric if using this.

- Include a lightweight and light-coloured fabric in your gatherings. This will be used for writing or tracing your words onto for stitching.

- You may wish to gather some papers with text and a selection of haberdashery items such as buttons.

- Take your time and enjoy this as a valuable part of the making process. Once you have a little collection, lay the pieces out so you can see them all together. From here, start to edit them and make your selection.

- Using a pencil, trace your motif onto a piece of tissue paper, keeping in mind the scale of your piece.

- Select your words for hand-stitching and write or trace these onto a piece of tracing paper.

STEP TWO: SELECTING

- In addition to my inkjet print and background fabric, for a small piece like this I generally choose three or four different main fabrics. After I have made this selection, I add a few contrasting fabrics to use in small amounts. I then consider the colour story that emerges and remove anything that doesn't fit.

- I then rip a selection of squares and rectangles in different sizes. I do this because I like to use raw edges and embrace the scrappy look with unravelling threads. I make an exception with my inkjet prints and cut these because the print rarely lies along the straight grain.

- Make the most of any features in your fabrics, such as buttonholes, hems, decorative stitching, darns and, of course, printed pattern.

Materials, words and motifs gathered when my head was immersed in thoughts of my mother-in-law and her wonderful recipes.

I've selected my materials, played around with the placement, and now have my final layout of fabric patches.

STEP THREE: PLAYING

- Now you can start playing around with the placement of your fabric 'patches'. Choose one as your starting point and place it on the background, but avoid positioning it bang in the centre. If I'm using inkjet-printed text, then this would usually be my starting point.

- Place any paper patches directly onto your background fabric.

- Start layering your other pieces around these, moving things around and creating interesting lines with your edges and corners.

- Be prepared that this process will take much longer than you think!

- You may need to rip some different sizes of fabric or substitute them, but nothing is wasted. Keep all your scraps, no matter how tiny.

- Think about where your stitched handwriting will go and make

sure you leave enough space. Also think about the positioning of your stitched drawing. Take your tissue paper tracing and try positioning it in different places – on a patch of its own, spanning more than one patch of fabric or, if it is bigger in scale, it could cover a large area of your collage.

- Add any extras such as buttons.

- Once you are happy with your layout, walk away and come back to it later. It's always good to return to something with fresh eyes.

- Trace your handwriting onto your fabric as described in Chapter Two. I do this by tracing the space created by my patches, then arranging the text to fit.

- Take a photo of your finished layout so you can refer to it later.

STEP FOUR:
ATTACHING YOUR FABRICS

At this point you can simply pin and tack your pieces in place. They will become attached later with your decorative stitching. However, I use Bondaweb to attach the bottom layer of my collage, including any paper patches, as I like them to lie really flat on the background. The downside of this method is that it adds more layers to stitch through.

To cut Bondaweb for fabric patches with ripped edges

• Carefully remove a patch, measure it and cut a piece of Bondaweb slightly smaller.

• Iron the Bondaweb onto the back of the fabric by placing the rough side of the Bondaweb onto the wrong side of the fabric. You'll have a tiny border all around – this preserves your lovely frayed edges.

• Leave it to cool, peel off the backing paper and put your patch back in place.

To cut Bondaweb for cut edges and paper patches

• Cut a piece of Bondaweb slightly oversized and iron it onto the back of your fabric or paper. Mark your cutting line either in pencil on the back or in erasable pen on the front.

To attach

• Remove any patches without Bondaweb and any buttons.

• Use a hot, dry iron to fix down your bottom layer. I cover my work with a piece of baking parchment to protect it. I keep checking that everything is still in place as I work.

• Pin and/or tack any remaining patches back in place.

• You can use Bondaweb on some of your larger patches on subsequent layers if you wish – I often do – but remember that this adds stiffness to your piece for stitching. You may also see the outlines of any patches underneath.

Words are traced onto fabric patches and pieces are attached. Stitching is started on my tissue paper motif.

LEFT: *John Patterson's Nana*, 17 × 24cm (6¾ × 9½in) Finished collage with words from Pat's recipes inkjet-printed onto calico and hand-stitched in a tiny backstitch.

OPPOSITE, ABOVE: *Miss Johnston*, 26 × 18cm (10¼ × 7 in). The recipe is the original, handwritten on paper, and the postcard is inkjet-printed onto calico. Both are emphasized by the blanket stitch edgings.

OPPOSITE, BELOW: *Bramble Jelly*, 16 × 24cm (6¼ × 9½ in). Create a series of collages by having things in common that run throughout the pieces. As well as working on the same theme, consider colour palette, background fabric, threads and stitching patterns.

STEP FIVE: STITCHING

Once you've selected your threads, it's time for hand-stitching.

- If you don't know where to start, thread your needle with one of your threads, choose one of your patches and sew all the way around the edge with a running stitch. I promise that as you are doing this, an idea will come to you as to what to do next.

- Working in this intuitive way, stepping back every so often to look at the full picture, you will soon see where you need a little contrasting colour or texture or where a colour needs to be repeated to create balance. Allow your stitching to be part of your own individual mark. Whether it's wild and uneven or perfectly formed, embrace it as your personal signature.

- Don't work all the way around the edge of every patch in one stitch. Think about extending lines of stitching beyond the edges of some, of leaving spaces and creating

groupings of stitches. This helps to unify your collage, encouraging the eye to move around the piece as a whole rather than seeing it as a series of individual patches. You can also use stitching to alter the appearance of patches. For example, a brightly coloured fabric can be toned down by covering it with a lighter-coloured filling stitch such as seed stitch.

- Sew your motif outlines relatively early on as they may influence the stitching of neighbouring patches. Leave stitching your paper patches until later when your collage is beginning to take shape. I frequently unpick and redo areas of stitching as I work, changing my mind as I go along, but paper is not forgiving if you need to unpick anything.

- Continue working until you are happy with the outcome, then press, using a cloth or piece of baking parchment to protect it. Take care if using steam around areas of paper.

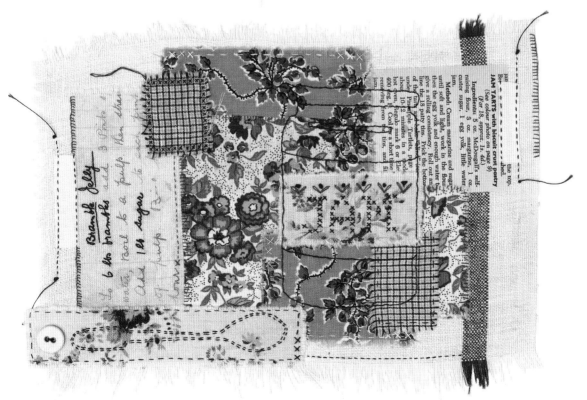

Maria Thomas

Meaningful materials, words and motifs are ever-present in artist Maria Thomas's work, as is the theme of home and family life.

Maria describes her work as being *'A celebration of our daily rituals and their associated ephemera that passes unnoticeably through our hands.'* It's inspired by the everyday, the overlooked and the domestic. She draws inspiration from the events of her life: memories and experiences are pieced and patched together using found papers, often food wrappers and packaging, as well as used fabrics and small objects.

Maria works intuitively using traditional Indian, patchwork and quilting methods, screen print and embroidery techniques, along with graphic fonts, texts, lists and words. She mixes everything together to create

LEFT: **Maria Thomas**, *Saturday*, **50 × 50cm (20 × 20in)**. Linen, cotton, silk and wool, worked with screenprint, *shishadar* (mirrorwork), kantha, appliqué, patchwork, hand- and machine-embroidery techniques. Detail shown below.

random patterns that suggest everyday narratives and moments in time.

Maria says: *'The basic elements of textiles are my trusted tools – screen print, embroidery and composition. They allow me to connect all the strands of my life together and enable a creative a handwriting that belongs to me.'*

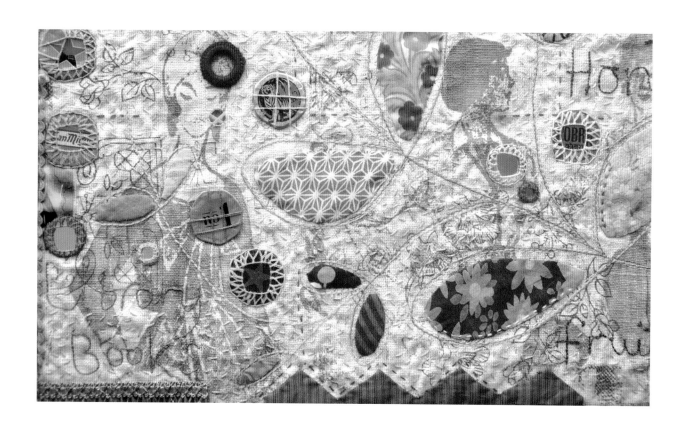

An envelope still life

I talked in Chapter One about the pile of letters and envelopes that seem to be a permanent fixture on my kitchen table and some of the memories that they invoke, so I decided to stitch a series of kitchen still lifes onto envelopes and postcards. The first sample that I made was stitched onto an ordinary envelope received through the post. I loved the idea, so decided to search for old and interesting envelopes or postcards to use as my backgrounds. I particularly look for interesting stamps and lovely names and/or addresses, though I deliberately obscure some of the address with my stitching. I then create small kitchen still lifes as my motifs using a combination of print, appliqué and stitch.

Jam Tarts, **12 × 11cm (4¾ × 4¼in).** I chose this envelope dated 1909 for its glorious handwritten address. Hand-stitched with one strand of embroidery cotton.

- Choose an envelope or postcard with interesting handwritten words. If using an envelope, I carefully tear the front from the back to give me one layer.

- Draw a small still life. My envelope is addressed to Rev. J. B. Duncan, so I rather liked the idea of him tucking into a plate of jam tarts at the vicarage.

- I was able to trace my motif onto the envelope. I used a FriXion pen, which erases when heat is applied.

- Protect the paper/card from perforating and tearing with your stitch holes by reinforcing the back. I do this by using a small piece of iron-on interfacing like that used in dressmaking. Iron this on the back to cover the area where your motif will be stitched. You could also use a glue stick to glue a patch of cotton on the back, but this is slightly bulkier to stitch through.

- I pierced stitching holes on my drawn line with my needle, then stitched my motif and some of the wonderful handwriting on the envelope. Don't make your stitches too small or the paper may perforate.

- Iron to erase your drawn line. Once again, I use baking parchment over my work to protect it.

Haf Weighton

In January 2022, while stuck at home recovering from Covid, artist Haf Weighton's attention turned to her kitchen.

Haf explains: '*The days were dark; I didn't feel like going out and I had lost my ability to taste food. I started drawing what I could see in front of me every day. Untidy drawers, food cupboards, dirty dishes stacked in piles, a butter dish and left-over fish and chips in paper. Food, cutlery, plates and packaging seemed to have a new meaning.*'

Haf posted her drawings online and was approached by Amgueddfa Cymru – Museum Wales to create a project on food, working with asylum seekers and refugees at Oasis Cardiff.

She was commissioned to work with Oasis clients to create a stitched tablecloth as part of the Refugee Wales (2019–23) project, funded by the Arts and Humanities Research Council. This piece depicts a series of hand- and machine-sewn plates of food spanning countries including Albania, Honduras, Morocco, Sudan and Syria. The work showcases the skills and creativity of those who contributed and symbolizes the act of coming together around the dinner table, to share as one community.

Haf says: '*Communication can take many forms. I have had many discussions while stitching at Oasis, often with people who don't speak the same languages as me. The shared process of stitching provided a platform for many discussions, sometimes with the aid of Google Translate, but sometimes just with smiles and understanding. I learnt about countries and cultures alien to me. I was honoured that many people shared their stories with me. In return, my new friends learnt about my Welshness and heard me speaking my mother tongue to colleagues who were assisting on the projects. The highlight of each workshop was the lunch we shared around the table while stitching. Volunteers who themselves were refugees or asylum seekers would bring their food to the table. I tasted food from many different cultures. The shared experience of eating and stitching was unique. The project became far more than the pieces we co-created. Through stitch, we created a community.*'

RIGHT: *Feast*, **255 × 221cm (100 × 87in).** Tablecloth stitched by clients of Oasis Cardiff with Haf Weighton. Drawing, fabric collage, hand- and machine-stitch. © Amgueddfa Cymru – Museum Wales. Detail shown on the left.

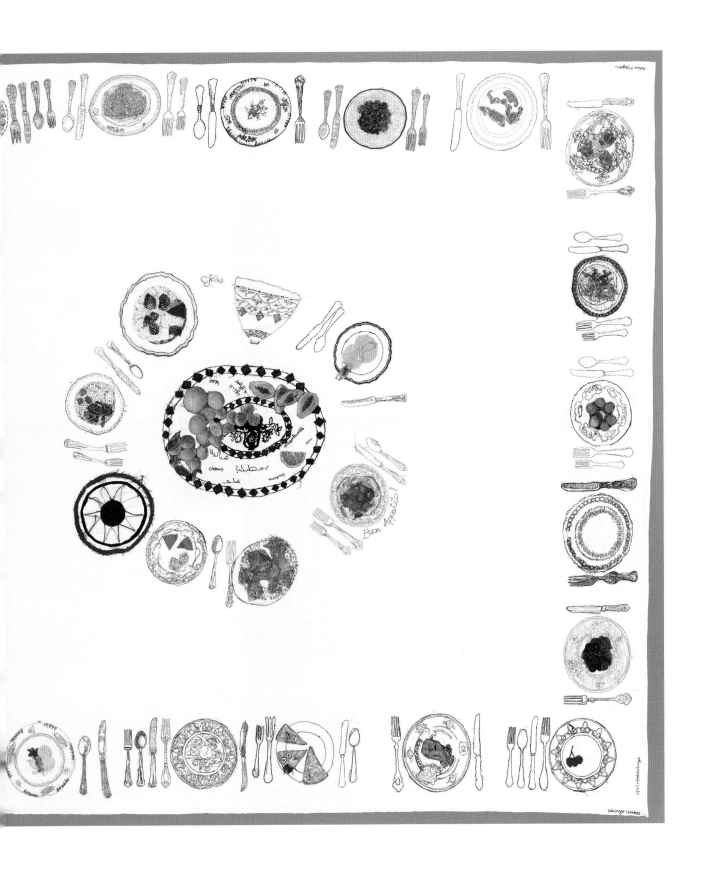

This project was made possible thanks to the
Arts and Humanities Research Council.

Stories from the Scullery

I chose the title for this chapter because 'scullery' is such a wonderful word! My inspiration is drawn from the cleaning side of kitchen duties, the 'chores', which leads inevitably to thinking about our domestic roles. However, your *threads of thought* may have taken you in completely different directions.

Scullery Threads of Thought

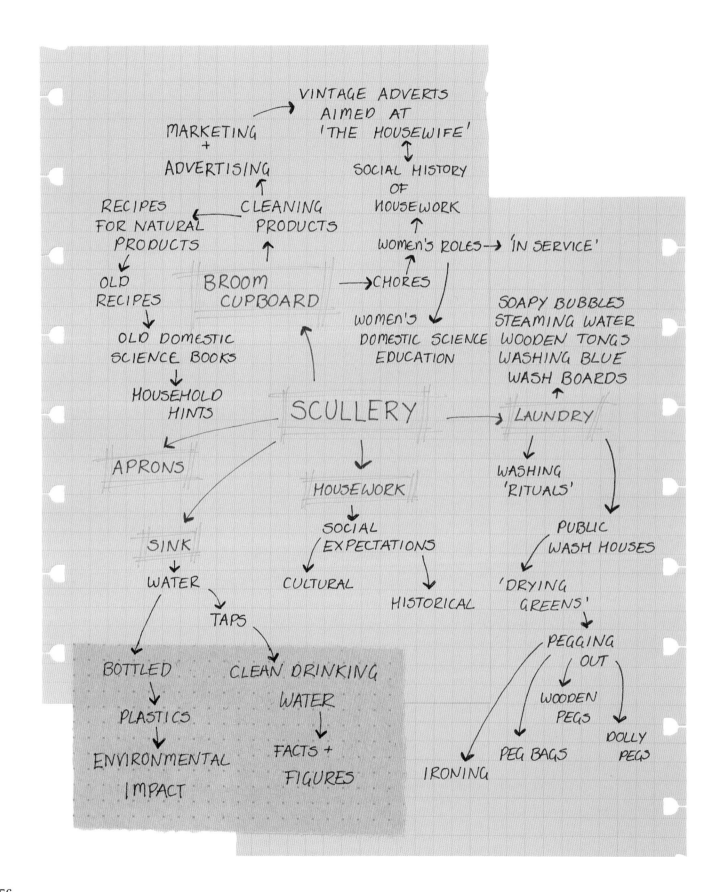

MARKETING + ADVERTISING → VINTAGE ADVERTS AIMED AT 'THE HOUSEWIFE'

VINTAGE ADVERTS AIMED AT 'THE HOUSEWIFE' ↕ SOCIAL HISTORY OF HOUSEWORK

RECIPES FOR NATURAL PRODUCTS ← CLEANING PRODUCTS

CLEANING PRODUCTS ↑ (to MARKETING + ADVERTISING)

SOCIAL HISTORY OF HOUSEWORK ↑ WOMEN'S ROLES → 'IN SERVICE'

RECIPES FOR NATURAL PRODUCTS ↓ OLD RECIPES

BROOM CUPBOARD

CHORES ↑ (to WOMEN'S ROLES)

OLD RECIPES ↓ OLD DOMESTIC SCIENCE BOOKS

WOMEN'S DOMESTIC SCIENCE EDUCATION

SOAPY BUBBLES
STEAMING WATER
WOODEN TONGS
WASHING BLUE
WASH BOARDS

OLD DOMESTIC SCIENCE BOOKS ↓ HOUSEHOLD HINTS

SCULLERY

LAUNDRY

HOUSEHOLD HINTS ↓ APRONS

HOUSEWORK

WASHING 'RITUALS'

SINK ↓ WATER

HOUSEWORK ↓ SOCIAL EXPECTATIONS

PUBLIC WASH HOUSES

WATER → BOTTLED
WATER → TAPS

SOCIAL EXPECTATIONS ↓ CULTURAL / HISTORICAL

'DRYING GREENS' ↓ PEGGING OUT

BOTTLED ↓ PLASTICS ↓ ENVIRONMENTAL IMPACT

CLEAN DRINKING WATER ↓ FACTS + FIGURES

PEGGING OUT ↓ WOODEN PEGS / PEG BAGS / DOLLY PEGS

IRONING

WORDS

Meaningful Materials

CALICO, MUSLIN, COTTON, LINEN

VINTAGE GRAIN-SACK COTTON

DISHCLOTHS

APRONS

OLD TEA TOWELS

VINTAGE MANGLE CLOTH

LAUNDRY:

    TABLECLOTHS

    SHEETING + BEDDING

    SHIRTING CLOTH

    SUMMER DRESS COTTONS

PAPERS: ADVERTS FROM OLD MAGAZINES

INSTRUCTIONS FROM OLD TEXTBOOKS

PERSONAL RECOLLECTIONS

RECIPES FOR HOME CLEANING PRODUCTS

LAUNDRY CARE LABELS

OLD DOMESTIC SCIENCE BOOKS

OLD HOUSEHOLD HINTS

ARTICLES FROM VINTAGE MAGAZINES

OLD MAGAZINE + TELEVISION ADVERTS

THINGS YOU DO:

WASH, HANG, SORT, IRON, FOLD, PUTAWAY

A.F. A.F. A.F.

Motifs

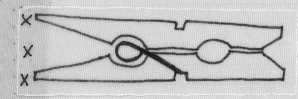

WASHING LINE, CLOTHES PEGS, WOODEN TONGS   LAUNDRY → BUTTONS

LAUNDRY SYMBOLS, IRON, COLLAR & CUFFS

DARNS & MENDS

LAUNDRY MARKS, LAUNDRY TAPES, STITCHED INITIALS

BRAND NAMES FROM VINTAGE ADVERTISING

AEROSOL CANS, TRIGGER SPRAY BOTTLES, POLISH TINS

BRUSHES

INGREDIENTS FOR CLEANING PRODUCTS → LAVENDER

PINE ↓ LEMON

Jo from a Tablecloth

1) Starch in boiling water starch in the proportion of 1-4.

2) Fold. a) Pull into shape.
   b) Fold in half right sides inside.

starch in the proportion of 1-4

Old Bleach
EL.451

15 ins.
No. 3067
EMBROIDERY LINEN
Ivory
An "OLD GLAMIS" Fabric

turn cloth end to end

Washday memories

My memories of Monday washday and helping my mum unload her twin tub washing machine led me down a rabbit hole of all things laundry-related. I often start my research on a theme by searching online and seeing what comes up. As well as finding informative articles on the social history of any subject, I also search on eBay or Etsy.

Over the years, the search term 'vintage laundry' has uncovered old 'domestic science' school books, washboards, lengths of vintage 'mangle cloth' (used to protect the clothing as it went through the rollers of the mangle), hand-carved wooden clothes pegs, and packets of 'washing blue'. These all become things to find out more about, or things to buy and use as reference or for words, motifs and even materials in themselves.

The packets of Reckitt's Blue were bought because so many people in my workshops reminisce about using these little bags of blue powder. They were designed to banish any hint of yellowing and leaving fabric 'whiter than white', as the advertising would have us believe. When I showed my husband, he immediately remembered as a child looking out for the 'blue men' whenever they passed the Reckitt's Dolly Blue factory in Cumbria in the north of England.

I love the inspiration that comes from handling items like these and the thought that they have been used over and over, sometimes in the most mundane of activities. This will often spark off more research. As I've said previously, you can find yourself captivated by stories far removed from your initial *threads of thought*.

OPPOSITE: *Old Bleach*, 27 × 35cm (10½ × 13¾in). Cloth collage with words inspired by old school notes giving instructions on how to iron. Motifs taken from old embroidery transfers.

RIGHT: Some of the laundry-related items in my collection. Just handling these items makes me wonder about their stories.

Cloth collages

These collages use the same making process as the small cloth collage in the previous chapter but are worked on larger background fabrics. You can, of course, use this same process to create collages exploring any theme.

Laundry tales

This project was inspired by an old domestic science jotter that was found in a charity shop and then very kindly gifted to me. It belonged to a girl named Patsy and its dates run between July 1943 and October 1945.

I don't know Patsy's age, but she had beautiful handwriting, so I'm guessing she was almost old enough to step out into the world of starching and ironing frilled pillowcases, of stiffening and polishing shirt collars, of making homemade soap and using laundry blue, and certainly old enough to know the rules of ironing. I'm sure she was up to the job, as she had clearly written out all her notes and regularly received 10/10 for her exercises. Charity shop finds such as this jotter can be a valuable resource and offer a fascinating glimpse into the social history of the time.

I created my own fabric by inkjet-printing one of the jotter pages, 'Preparations for Washing', onto an unbleached cotton fabric. I chose to use a beautiful piece of vintage linen mangle cloth as my foundation fabric. I then gathered together a selection of vintage materials, including shirting

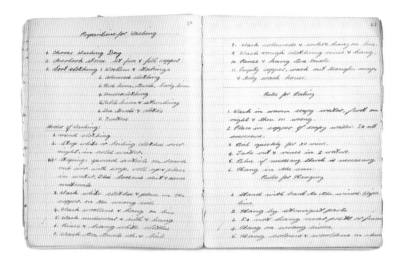

fabrics of different textures. When using parts of old garments, I always look for interesting shapes, such as the round neckline of the striped shirt. I unpick seams and tear fabric pieces, making the most of features such as buttonholes. I used old wooden clothes pegs and tongs as my motifs and stitched these with a simple running stitch worked in two strands of stranded cotton.

I chose to highlight certain words from the jotter text by backstitching over the printed text. I also included old linen laundry buttons and name tapes found at an antique fair. I often use other people's names and initials in my work as a lovely way to add a snippet of someone else's story. The small blue checked patches are added as a nod to my granda and his working shirts. You'll notice that I include them in several of my collages, and I just can't resist stitching a cross into the squares!

ABOVE: One of my favourite pages in this old jotter, I've used these words in several of my cloth collages.

OPPOSITE: *Laundry Tales,* **30 × 30cm (12 × 12in).** Used, washed and worn fabrics collaged onto a vintage mangle cloth background with hand-stitching.

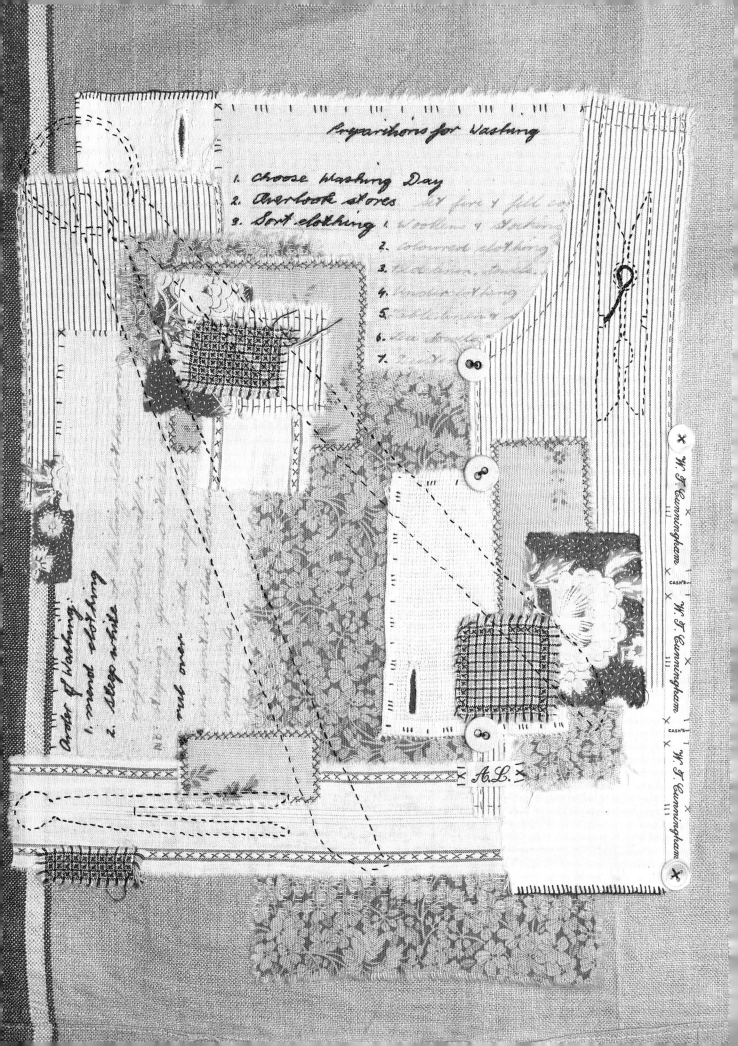

1. Dust furniture, covering large articles & removing smaller ones

2. Clean flues the night before if possible

3. Dust walls, high ledges, pictures & doors

4. Sweep floor keeping doors & windows shut

5. Scrub tables & then floor

6. Remove dust sheets, dust furniture & rearrange the room

Weekly Cleaning of Kitchen

7. Clean windows

Clean, dust, sweep, scrub

This collage was inspired by some school domestic science notes that a friend gifted to me. They were written by her gran Annie McLean, who was born in 1897. I made a tracing of Annie's handwritten notes on the 'Weekly Cleaning of Kitchen' and then stitched them in backstitch.

I used an old woollen blanket as my foundation fabric. The fabrics for my main patches all came from one old quilt, and I rather love the unusual but authentic colour combination that results. When my mum was a child, quilts and coverings were patched together from what was available without too much concern as to whether the colours complemented each other or not! I've left some of the original seams of the quilt intact and unpicked others, leaving the old stitching lines visible.

I laid out my fabric patches onto my background, paying particular attention to creating interesting lines around the outer edges. I then trimmed any exposed blanket backing away to create the irregular outline.

I decided to use old cleaning products for my motifs. I created the very simple shape of a bar of household soap, using the simple appliqué method discussed in Chapter Two and an old patch of feed sack fabric. I chose green because of memories of Fairy soap, which was always green and would be rubbed into stains before washing and along the fold lines of collars and cuffs. I stitched the soap bubbles in seed stitch, as a reminder of the hot soapy water in my mum's twin tub washing machine.

I traced around a picture I found online of an old tin of Brasso and stitched it in a single strand of embroidery cotton. The letters in the words 'scrub' and 'clean' are stitched following one of my vintage cross-stitch alphabet patterns. I'm not too precise with my stitching, so the crosses don't always line up. However, I like to reinterpret techniques, especially when they are taken from old domestic science school books where precision was key and rules and instructions were not to be argued with!

Clean, Dust, Sweep, Scrub, **25 × 36cm (10 × 14in).** Cloth collage with hand-stitching. I love that the words offer a glimpse into domestic routines of ordinary households in the early 20th century.

Vanessa Marr

Artist and academic Vanessa Marr began making art with dusters back in 2014 when she was researching the domestic origins of fairy tales.

She discovered that women told each other fairy tales while they worked, often with cloth, so she sought out a cloth object that could embody these narratives. She selected a bright yellow duster because its relationship with domesticity is immediately recognizable and, as a cheap, undervalued item that likely lives under the kitchen sink, it shares the invisible nature of so-called 'women's work'.

Vanessa explains: *'My first piece of work with the dusters,* Promises and Expectations, *subverted the fairy-tale promises made to women and girls, such as "happily ever after", with images relating to cloth and gendered subjection.'*

This inspired Vanessa's collaborative arts project *Women & Domesticity – What's Your Perspective?* Here she invites women to embroider their own stories onto dusters using words or motifs that illustrate their domestic experiences. They explore themes such as memory, mothering, domestic violence, caring, home and homelessness, celebration and frustration. The collection, including hundreds of stitched dusters, has been exhibited across the UK as well as in mainland Europe and the USA.

Vanessa says: *'The possibilities of this simple cloth endlessly connect me to my desire to stitch by hand, tell stories, and entice conversations about the lives of everyday women in their homes.'*

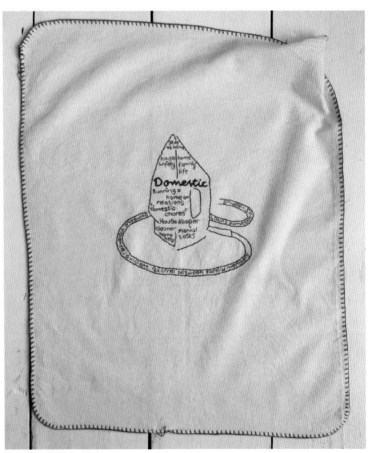

Vanessa Marr, *Promises and Expectations*, 30 × 40cm (12 × 16in). Seven hand-embroidered cleaning cloths commenting upon the expectations of women within a domestic environment. Not only does Vanessa use motifs such as the iron, but the dusters are a powerful motif in themselves.

Expanding the idea of 'motifs'

While using the three elements of meaningful materials, words and motifs is a great starting point for creating personal stitched stories, it is simply that: a way to get started with your ideas. In my own work I'd certainly always use materials that are meaningful in some way, but of course not every piece of work needs to include words or a stitched motif or drawing.

You can expand your idea of motifs to include anything that will help illustrate your story; for example, the shape of your finished piece, or perhaps how you mount it.

Maria Thomas

Artist Maria Thomas uses the apron or 'pinny' as her motif to honour part of her family history. *Annie Violet* is one piece from her series *Seven Sisters*, featuring seven apron-shaped hangings based on her great-aunties and grandmothers (the seven sisters of the title). Maria's Great-Auntie Annie went to work at the 'Big House' when she was just fourteen years old. Maria recalls that her Welsh grandmother, or Mamgu, often described her older sister Annie as being 'lucky' in having gained a position 'in service'.

Maria was fascinated by this older generation of women and the family tradition of shared recipes, letter-writing and sewing. Her aim was to create an atmosphere of her memories of her relatives, with each 'pinny' being a response to their individual character.

Maria says: *'Using original text from my family's shared recipes, I cherished the opportunity to hold hands with the women of my past while making memory keepers all blended together with their writing and my stitch.'*

Maria Thomas, *Annie Violet*, 50 × 110cm (19¾ × 43½in). Re-worked vintage tablecloth with a mix of linen, cotton, paper and haberdashery, worked with hand patchwork and image transfer techniques.

Informal display ideas

I tend to take an informal approach to displaying my finished work.

I love using tiny bulldog clips that I attach to the top of my work and hang from a nail in the wall.

I also use wooden clipboards as an informal display method. You can display a grouping of clipboards on your walls and then easily swap the pieces you are showing.

Artists' deep-edge canvases can also be a great way to mount cloth collages. I don't like the finish of the canvas surface, so I cover them with fabric, usually an unbleached cotton. You can also add decorative features around the edges of the canvas if you wish, or continue lines of stitching from your collage onto your covering fabric before you attach it to the canvas.

Be on the lookout for interesting clips and clipboards that you could use as a means of informal display.

Motifs as display

My chosen method of display is often inspired by my *threads of thought* so the display itself forms part of the motif.

Go back to your *threads of thought* with display in mind and see what you come up with.

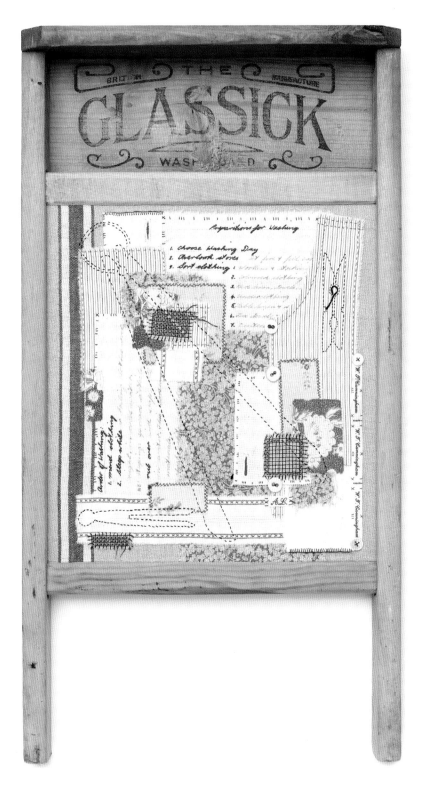

Laundry Tales,
32 × 60cm
(12½ × 24in).
I searched for vintage washboards that I could use as a frame and then created the collage pictured on page 61 to fit within it.

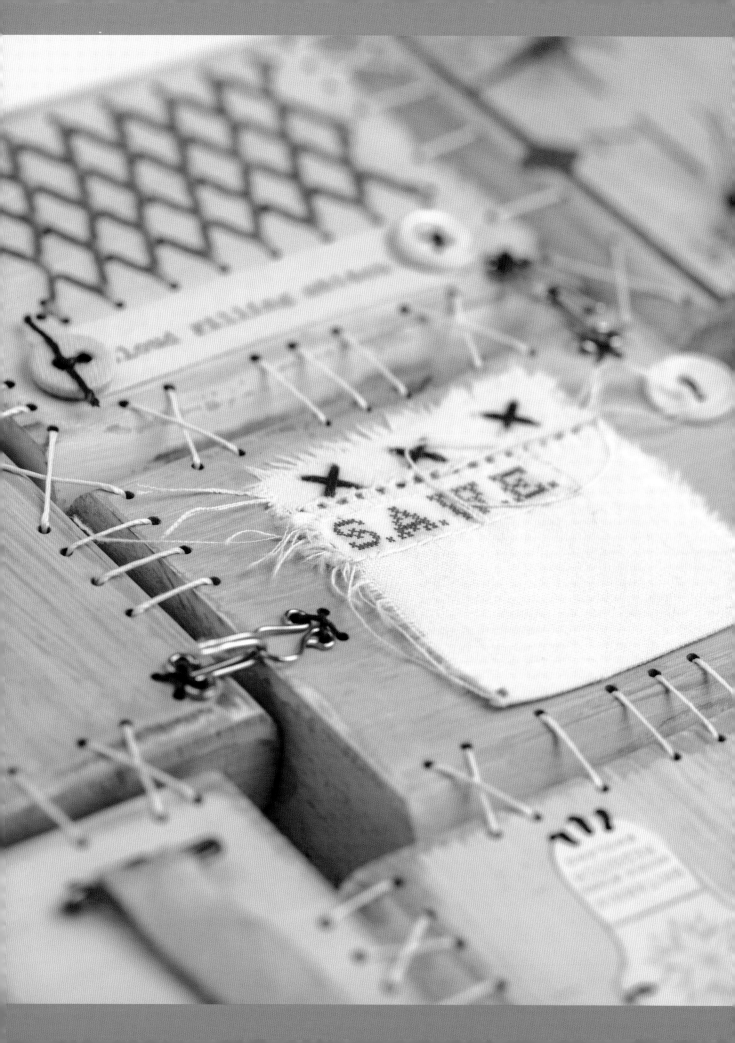

Stories from the Snug

I chose the title of this chapter because of the wonderful feelings the word 'snug' conjures: warmth, security and shutting out the rest of the world. However, you could change the title if you wish to work in a different direction.

My attention for this chapter was particularly drawn to the fireside, the activities that take place there and the people who sit around it – and, rather oddly, to the sideboard in my childhood home.

Snug Threads of Thought

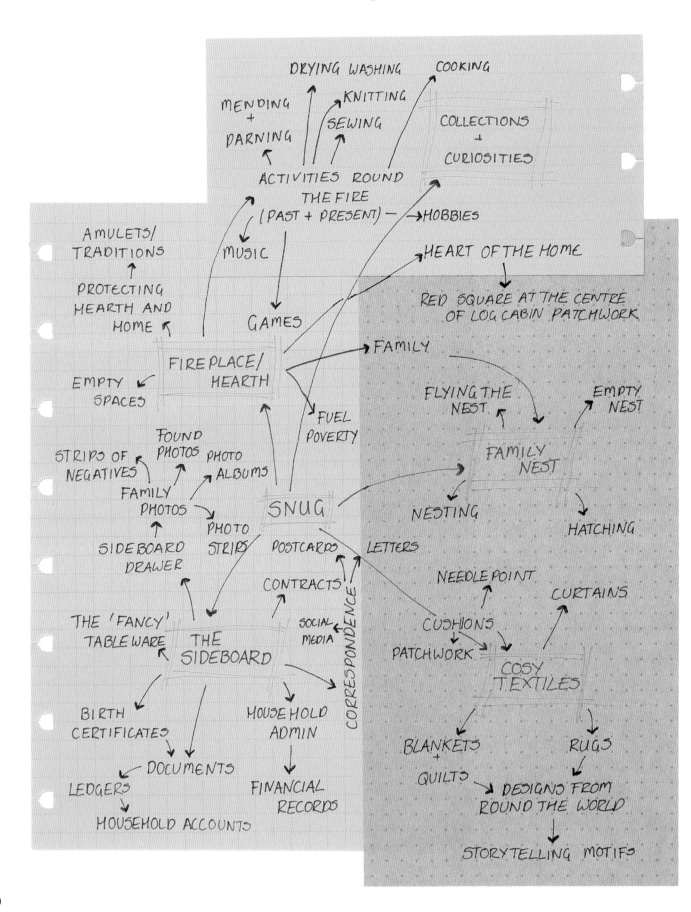

DRYING WASHING

COOKING

MENDING + DARNING

KNITTING

SEWING

COLLECTIONS + CURIOSITIES

ACTIVITIES ROUND THE FIRE (PAST + PRESENT) —→ HOBBIES

AMULETS/ TRADITIONS

MUSIC

HEART OF THE HOME

PROTECTING HEARTH AND HOME

RED SQUARE AT THE CENTRE OF LOG CABIN PATCHWORK

GAMES

FAMILY

FIREPLACE/ HEARTH

FLYING THE NEST

EMPTY NEST

EMPTY SPACES

FUEL POVERTY

FOUND PHOTOS

STRIPS OF NEGATIVES

PHOTO ALBUMS

FAMILY NEST

FAMILY PHOTOS

NESTING

HATCHING

SIDEBOARD DRAWER

PHOTO STRIPS

SNUG

POSTCARDS

LETTERS

NEEDLE POINT

CONTRACTS

CURTAINS

THE 'FANCY' TABLEWARE

SOCIAL MEDIA

CORRESPONDENCE

CUSHIONS

THE SIDEBOARD

PATCHWORK

COSY TEXTILES

BIRTH CERTIFICATES

HOUSEHOLD ADMIN

BLANKETS + QUILTS

RUGS

DOCUMENTS

LEDGERS

FINANCIAL RECORDS

DESIGNS FROM ROUND THE WORLD

HOUSEHOLD ACCOUNTS

STORYTELLING MOTIFS

Meaningful Materials

COSY + COMFORTING WITH A
                'LIVED IN' FEEL

OLD WOOLLEN BLANKETS

LOG CABIN QUILTS

PATCHWORK + NEEDLEPOINT

WORN + WASHED COTTONS

FADED FURNISHINGS

MENDS + DARNS

CHINTZY PATTERNS

LACE DOILIES + ANTIMACASSARS

PAPERS:

      OLD DOCUMENTS

      PHOTOGRAPHS

      OLD LETTERS

      KNITTING PATTERNS

      HABERDASHERY ON CARDS

      OLD MAGAZINE + BOOK PAGES

WORDS

PERSONAL MEMORIES

REMEMBERED CONVERSATIONS

WORDS ASSOCIATED WITH FAMILY

OLD DOCUMENTS

BANK STATEMENTS

HOUSEHOLD ACCOUNTS

OLD LETTERS - PERSONAL +
                    FOUND

X Motifs X

FAMILY PHOTOS

STITCHED PORTRAITS

NESTS

CLOCKS & PICTURE FRAMES

TOASTING FORK

MUSICAL SCORES & INSTRUMENTS

HOBBIES & PASTIMES:

MOTIFS FROM
PATCHWORK &
   NEEDLEWORK

      SCISSORS

      THREAD REELS & CARDS

      BUTTON BOX

      PLAYING CARDS

      DOMINOS & JIGSAWS

      BOARD GAMES & DICE

      NEWSPAPER & CROSSWORDS

The sideboard: a snapshot of family life

Behind one door of our sideboard was a stack of dishes and plates, stored neatly, kept for best and thus never used. But behind the other door bulged the domestic admin of life: bank statements, household bills, receipts, used chequebooks with records of spending, and formal-looking papers documenting births, marriages and achievements.

The drawers housed photographs kept in envelopes with negatives tucked in pockets, school report cards, personal correspondence and the random 'stuff' that gets stuck in a drawer because there is nowhere else to put it. I love the thought that our social history can be pieced together by historians searching through everyday documents such as these, and that hints of my family's stories can be gleaned by simply thumbing through the well-worn pages stashed in untidy piles behind the sideboard doors.

These memories inspired me to gather together a number of family photos and to rummage through my small collection of old letters and correspondence – meaningful materials, wonderful words and motifs all in one!

Beeswax and brown paper

I first experimented with beeswax many years ago, coating papers and different fabrics, scraps of things that happened to be lying around my studio at the time. Time spent exploring with no end result in mind is never wasted. I can't emphasize enough the value of playing around and asking, 'What would happen if ...?'

I discovered that paper not only takes on a wonderfully tactile sheen, but also becomes translucent or transparent depending on its thickness. If the paper is printed on both sides then both become visible. This is particularly effective with handwriting, where the two sides merge to create an entirely new pattern, still legible if the viewer leans in and takes time to decipher it.

I also discovered that black-and-white photographs printed on paper take on the quality of the strips of negatives found in old packets of photos when they are coated in wax and held up to the light. I particularly loved the effect of printing photos on my favourite brown parcel paper.

OPPOSITE, LEFT:
Dear Son, 17 × 21cm (6¾ × 8¼in).
A waxed Second World War airmail letter is collaged with scraps of fabric and a black-and-white photo before being hand-stitched.

RIGHT: This black-and-white photo of my mum (bottom) is printed onto brown parcel paper, then waxed, then onto vellum and calico.

Photo strips

This project was inspired by packets of small black-and-white photos and memories of photo-booth strips marking afternoons in the 'big city' with my teenage pals. They look great hung in the window, memories wafting gently in the breeze.

You'll need:
- Beeswax or soy wax pellets
- Brown parcel paper cut to fit through your printer. I use the thicker paper bought in sheet form as I can't get parcel paper bought on a roll to feed through my printer.
- Baking parchment
- An old iron or craft iron
- An ironing pad and a wad of scrap paper
- Hooks and eyes
- Thread for stitching and decorative buttons if you wish

- Scan your photos onto your computer and enhance in photo software if you wish. Arrange them onto a page, leaving a sizeable border around each. You could use the actual photos and arrange these on your copier bed to photocopy if you prefer.

- Run a test print and then print onto the matte side of the brown paper.

- Tear or cut around each photo, leaving a small border.

- Cut a large sheet of baking parchment and put this on your ironing pad. I put several flat layers of reused paper underneath to protect my pad. Arrange two or three prints on top, keeping them away from the edge of the baking parchment.

- Sprinkle the prints with a few wax pellets and cover over with a double layer of baking parchment.

- Iron over the baking parchment until the wax melts and is absorbed into the brown paper. Take care not to let the wax escape from the edges of the parchment.

- You can add more pellets and repeat if your prints aren't completely coated.

- Repeat for all your prints and then arrange them in a strip. I joined my prints together with hooks and eyes, which allow them to move when hanging.

- Add decorative stitching, remembering that the back of your stitches will be seen when you hang the piece in the light. I tend to start my stitching with a knot on the front of the print as anything on the back will be visible.

- Working on a flat surface, I plan and pierce holes with my needle before actually stitching. It's ideal if you have a piece of foam board so that you can pierce the stitching holes without having to lift up your print.

- Line up your hooks and eyes carefully.

- I hang my piece from a small bulldog clip.

RIGHT: Photo strip, 8 × 38cm (3 × 15in). Old family photos printed onto parcel paper and waxed. This wafts gently in the breeze as it hangs from my window.

OPPOSITE: (detail) The paper becomes translucent so you can see both the front and the back of the stitching.

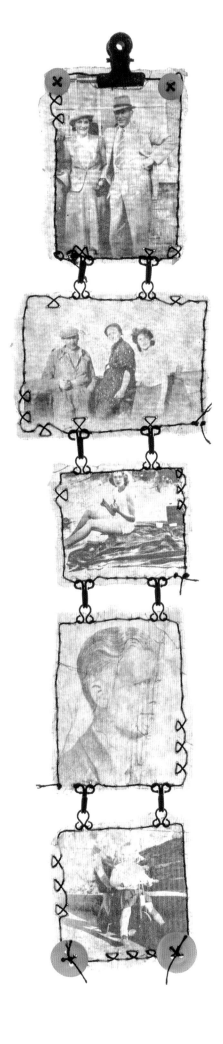

Other options

- You could simply print your photos onto a sheet of vellum and then stitch as above. As before, the back of your stitches will be visible, so keep this in mind when planning.

- You could print onto a sheet of cotton using an inkjet printer and the same method as outlined in Chapter Three. I then used Bondaweb to back my prints onto a cotton quilt batting before cutting out. You can be more adventurous with your decorative stitching when working with fabric, so I've added tiny crosses and buttonhole stitches along some of the edges. Again, I create little patterns of stitches instead of using one stitch all the way round.

The same family photos were used to create photo strip samples printed onto calico and vellum (far right).

Tina Gilmore

Tina is a mixed media artist who creates collage art and narrative assemblage from her vast collection of vintage ephemera.

Tina found the materials for *Dwelling on the Past* in a beautiful battered old leather suitcase, filled with 'one-hundred-year-old' mortgage documents and receipts, at an auction she attended with her antique dealer husband.

Tina says: *'Like its contents, the case was beautifully worn and frayed. The well-thumbed, aged, creased and smudged papers covered in tiny handwritten notes to bygone employees and clients filled my heart with joy. As I held and read the pages, they triggered fragments of memories from my own past about home and what it meant.'*

The abstract form of the house and its foundations sit quietly askew on the page, the woman placed to the side, seemingly nurturing and protecting it and its occupants.

Tina explains: *'My intention was to invite the viewer to think about who lives here. What does the façade of the house hide? What secrets are hidden in the contents of its drawers and cupboards? Does the idea of home endure on its own merit or is it helped along by the subtle nurturing of its forgotten "dwellers" of past times?'*

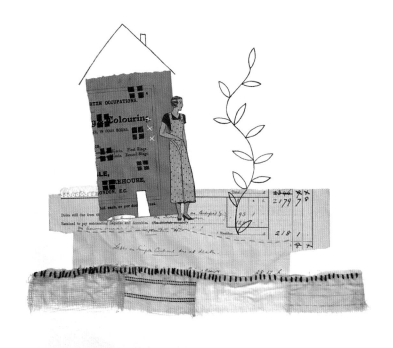

ABOVE RIGHT: Tina Gilmore, *Dwelling on the Past*, 32 × 38cm (12½ × 15in). Vintage found ephemera and fabrics collaged on paper background with ink drawing and hand-stitching.

RIGHT: Tina Gilmore, *Dwelling on the Past*, 29 × 39cm (11½ × 15½in). Vintage found ephemera and fabrics collaged on paper background with ink drawing and hand-stitching.

Wonky patchwork portraits

This was inspired by cosy log cabin quilts and 'courthouse steps' quilt blocks.

Traditionally, the log cabin is created around a central red square representing the fireplace or hearth, at the heart of the home. I've reinterpreted this by putting family at the heart of these pieces by using more of the old photographs that were stashed in our sideboard drawer and printing them onto fabric with my inkjet printer.

My words come from phrases used by my granny and granda and from handwritten recipes for traditional Scots food that my granny would have cooked regularly.

ABOVE LEFT: *Scotch Broth*, 21 × 27cm (8¼ × 10½in). This photo of my granny makes a wonderful central motif. The words come from a recipe for Scotch broth.

ABOVE: *Pea Soup*, 26 × 30cm (10¼ × 12in). I use many of the same fabrics across these two pieces, allowing them to sit together as part of a series.

Taking inspiration from your snug *threads of thought*, gather together a collection of meaningful materials for the strips. Cotton and linens are perfect, but you can also use papers if you wish. The beauty of this wonky style is that you can be inventive and use up the smallest of scraps.

I printed my photos onto commercially produced cotton fabric sheets. These are paper-backed and ready to be fed straight through the inkjet printer following the manufacturer's instructions.

After printing, leave a 1cm (³/₈in) border all round your photo and cut out. Place it in the centre of your foundation fabric and attach using Bondaweb so that it will lie flat, or simply tack it in place. I like to use cotton quilt batting as a foundation, but a piece of old sheeting or table linen works equally well.

This wonky style embraces uneven strips and raw edges and doesn't follow traditional rules for patchwork, but it is based loosely on a courthouse steps quilt block.

- Cut or rip the first strip the length of the bottom edge of your photo, place it face down on the photo and stitch 5mm (¼in) from the edge. Fold the strip back and press. (1)

- Strip two is done in the same way along the top edge. (2)

- Strip three is placed along the side edge of your photo overlapping strips 1 and 2. (3)

- Follow diagram 4 and continue working in this way. I usually do at least two rounds following this pattern and then start working more loosely. The diagram shows evenly sized strips, but the shape will quickly start to distort if you add different widths of strips.

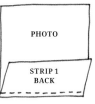

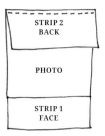

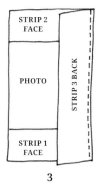

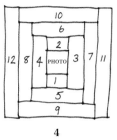

Sample showing the first few rows of patchwork. At this point I like to add some of the variations described on the next page.

Variations

- Vary the width of your strips, making sure that the overall look of the piece is balanced.

- Join fabrics together to create strips. Simply overlap the strips and stitch.

- Trace words onto your strip beforehand and then stitch them later.

- Add small patches into your stitched seams.

- Use paper for some strips. If the paper is fragile, reinforce it by first ironing it onto interfacing.

- Include lovely edges on your strips – edges of hankies, table linens, perhaps even curved edges from collars or beautifully frayed edges. Don't follow diagram 4 too rigidly; be led by the shapes of the strips.

Once you've completed your patchwork strips, add decorative stitching over some of the edges and stitch your words if you have included any. Use any of the techniques from previous chapters. A motif outline could look lovely, for example.

'She's aye been a gallus quine'

This is Scots for 'she's always been a spirited young woman'.

I added patches from an old feed sack quilt and finished off my piece by attaching it with cross stitches to a vintage quilt background. The photo is of my mum and gran, taken in a studio – hence the formal pose. There was no room in their country working lives for frivolities such as red ribbons and shoes, but I know my mum would've loved them, so I added them with stitch!

She's Aye Been a Gallus Quine, **23 × 33cm (9 × 13in).** My granda proudly described my mum as a 'gallus quine'. If you use personal words, you can create work that is particularly poignant.

She's aye been a gallus quine

... aye milam

8162/1

a dream of red shoes

Portraits without pictures

Think of other ways in which you could create portraits of people without using photographs and use that as your central square for a wonky patchwork portrait.

I made this series by stitching my granny's sayings at the heart of each piece as a way to keep her language and some of her sayings alive. My granny lived all her life in the Mearns in Aberdeenshire in the north-east of Scotland, but my mum moved away when she got married, as did I, so these wonderful words have become less familiar to our family over time. However, over recent years my mum has taken to using my granny's phrases again. Each time she does, I scribble them down for safe keeping. Because hand-stitching is so time-consuming, it feels to me like a very apt way to preserve and value other people's words.

OPPOSITE: *Open Yer Moo*, 21 × 21cm (8¼ × 8¼in). 'Ye just open yer moo [open your mouth] and let yer belly rumble', my granny's way of telling you that you're talking rubbish!

OPPOSITE, BELOW: *Nae a Lot*, 22 × 22cm (8½ × 8½in). 'There's nae a lot coming o'er me'. This was my mum's stock phrase during lockdown, in other words, 'I don't have anything to complain about!'

LEFT: *Aye a Sumthing*, 21 × 23cm (8¼ × 9in). 'Aye a sumthing' – usually said with a sigh and general acceptance of things going wrong! 'And that's an end tae't' – my granny always had the last word!

Fireside activities

I'll always associate my mum with making – embroidery, dressmaking, knitting and many other crafts. Her childhood was spent living, and working, on a croft in Aberdeenshire. Visits to the shops were rare and always a last resort. When something was needed, the first thought was always to make it. She tells stories of hooking rag rugs with her mum and dad during the winter months, a joint activity that brought them together around the fire. It was a case of 'needs must', using old sacking and discarded scraps of fabric to create colour and warmth, but still fondly remembered as precious time spent together.

My snug *threads of thought* reminded me of these stories, highlighting my own association of the fireplace with the sewing basket. I think of knitting jumpers, sewing on buttons, stitching labels onto school uniforms, of mending, darning, making things beautiful and of making beautiful things.

I grew up with the tools of these activities all around me. This may have fuelled my passion for sewing paraphernalia and the beauty of vintage packaging, such as old needle packets and button cards. For me, hunting through a box of vintage haberdashery unlocks countless memories and stories that come back to life as I handle each insignificant treasure.

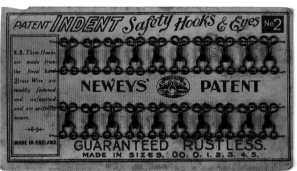

ABOVE AND LEFT: Vintage haberdashery items collected for the beauty of the packaging and the stories they bring to mind.

OPPOSITE: *Good Work into Good Materials*, **58 × 30cm (23 × 12in).** Collected vintage haberdashery items, old fabric scraps and wood.

Patchwood samplers: curated collections

These samplers celebrate the humble 'sewing box', a collection of commonplace items that were in daily use by our mothers and grandmothers as they performed their domestic chores. These indispensable objects played a vital role in eking out the household budget, striving to make things last a little longer, keeping families clothed and, of course, adorning household textiles and making them a little more beautiful.

I created my first patchwood samplers while exploring domestic gender roles. I wanted to combine the stereotypically 'female' role of sewing, mending and darning with a 'masculine' material, and chose wood. My original pieces were made from repurposed bed slats, playing on the words 'making the bed'. Exploring meaningful materials really can take you in unexpected directions!

Over the years I've developed these into carefully curated collections of personal and meaningful 'stuff' of any kind. The most mundane objects are layered and stitched onto cut and painted 'patches' of wood. Each patch is then hand-stitched together to create a unique patchwood sampler.

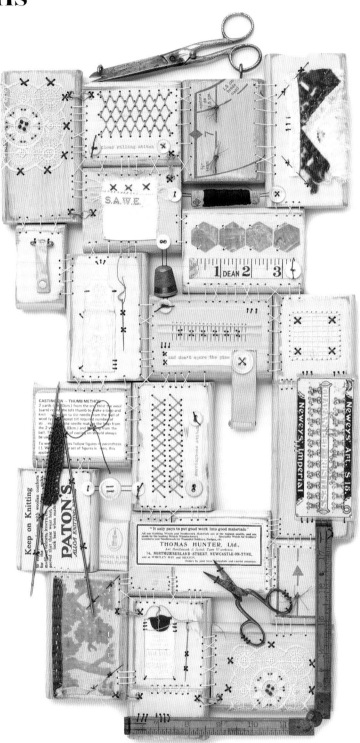

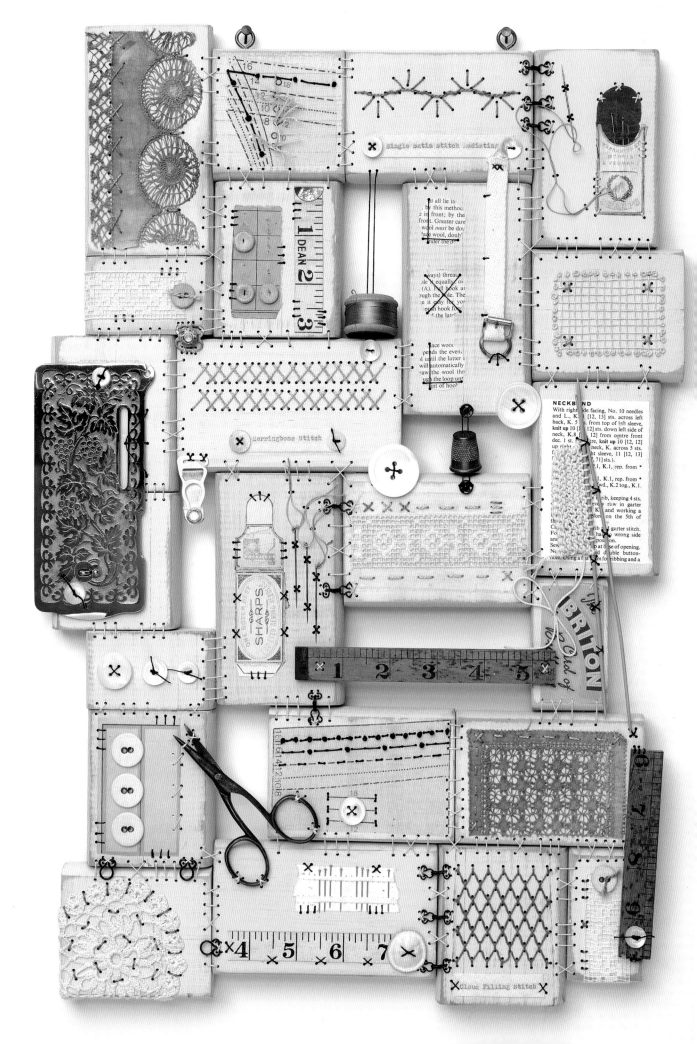

The tools and equipment for these aren't what you would find in most stitchers' workboxes, but they are great fun to make if you have some woodworking skills and a small electric drill such as a Dremel.

Each sampler is unique and will have different challenges. Therefore, I can't give step-by-step instructions, but here are some pointers if you wish to have a go.

- You'll need a small drill with a stand. The stand is important for safety and accuracy. The drill needs to take a 1.5mm diameter drill bit. A Dremel with workstation is ideal.

- Smooth planed timber from the DIY store is perfect for your patches.

- I use an electric mitre saw, but a handsaw and mitre box work fine. Always sand your cut edges to remove sharp splinters.

- I paint my patches with two coats of emulsion paint, often a darker base with a light-coloured top coat. Once the paint is dry, I sand it, taking it back to the wood in places.

- Work on a flat surface to arrange your patches. Make sure your layout will be structurally sound.

- Once you have a layout you like, start placing your collected items onto your patches. One item could overlap a couple of patches, overlap an edge or hang in a space.

- To join your patches, mark the position of your drilling holes for your stitches with a soft pencil. I create patterns of straight and cross stitches (diagram 1).

- Take a photo of your layout as you will need to remove items as you work.

- I glue my patches together with wood glue, leaving them to dry overnight. Larger samplers have to be made in sections. Work over a sheet of polythene.

ABOVE: Diagram 1, showing the placement of drill holes for the stitched pattern shown in red.

BELOW: I use John James bookbinders needles size 18 for stitching and a bradawl to mark the placement of objects.

OPPOSITE: *Lilac Patchwood*, **34 × 51cm (13½ × 20in).** Collected vintage haberdashery and sewing items, old fabric scraps and wood. The embroidery samples are all stitched through the wood.

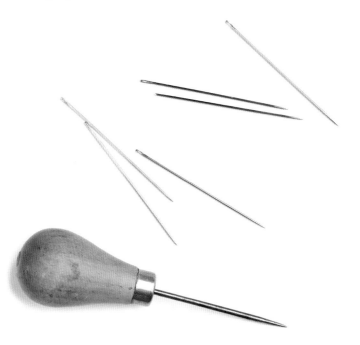

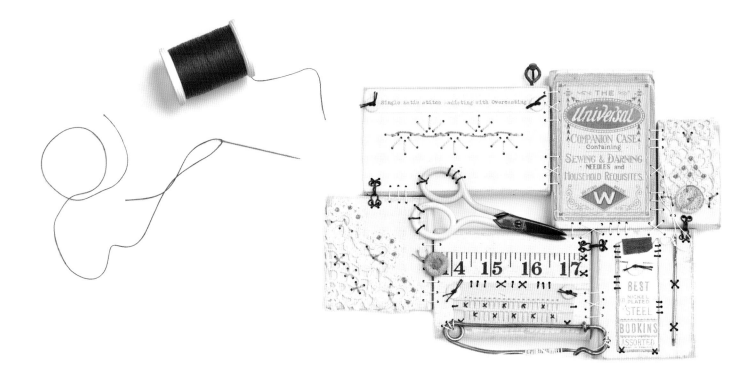

- Always test your drilling on a sample piece of the same wood. I use a 1.5mm drill bit.

- Take care when drilling. Hold the wood at all times and be aware of where your hands are placed. Sand the back to get rid of splinters.

- Use a strong, smooth thread for stitching. I use a linen bookbinding thread and bookbinder's needles.

- You'll need to work out how to attach each of your items individually. Some items, such as scissors and buttons, can be held in place simply by stitching. Use a pencil or bradawl to mark where to drill holes.

- I glue flat items such as button cards before stitching. I prefer to mark my stitching holes and drill before gluing things down. The sharp point of a bradawl will make a mark through cardboard.

- I use bookbinder's linen for most of my work, but you can use embroidery thread for decorative stitching.

One of the things I love about creating these is the problem-solving challenges throughout. You'll need to consider how your sampler will hang, how best to use precious items (probably not by drilling a hole through them) and how to securely attach awkward shapes. If you start with the basics of joining the patches, working out your stitching, drilling holes and stitching them together, this gives you the experience and confidence to work out your next steps.

Warning: This activity is highly addictive!

ABOVE: *Universal Companion*, 26 × 18cm (10¼ × 7in). Curated collection of vintage haberdashery stitched onto wood. Meaningful materials, words and motifs abound in these pieces.

ABOVE LEFT: I use 3-ply non waxed linen thread for stitching. It's available in a variety of colours.

**Personal sampler,
16 × 31cm (6½ ×
12¼in).** A collection
of personal
treasures including
my children's
drawings, an old
letter from my
student days and an
incense stick from
my wedding.

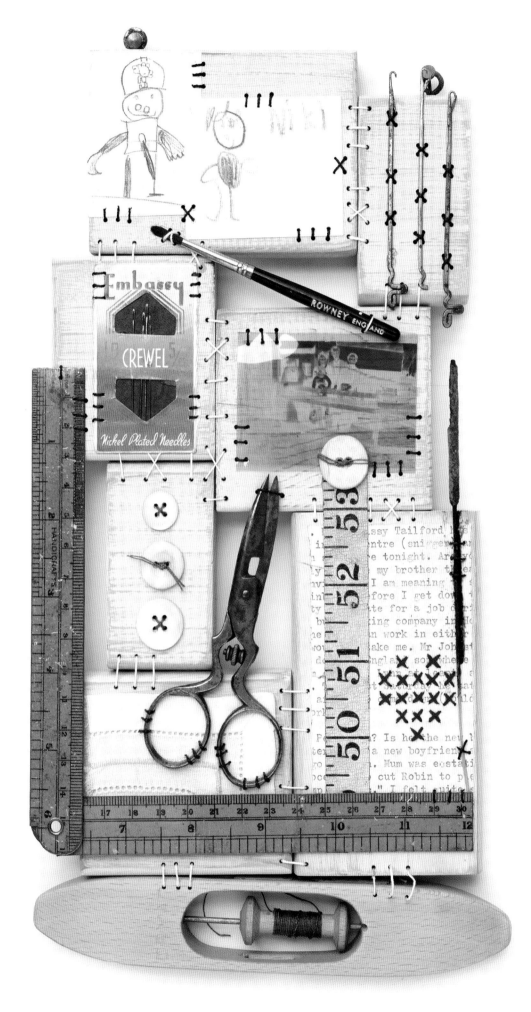

Name This Child

Name This Child

PAUL was first given as a ...
to a member of a famous Roman
family who was small in stature. It ...
It was a nickname. It ...
"the little one." ...
Then it became a big ...
... it was adopted ...
... who bec... ...

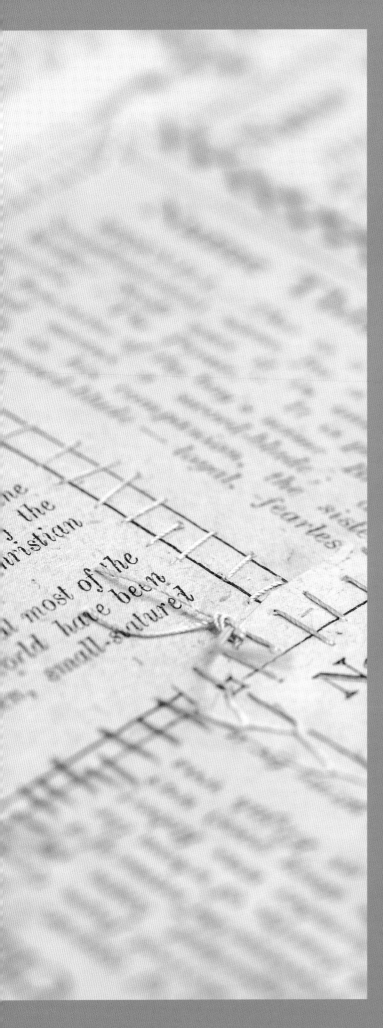

Nursery Tales

There are many potential areas to explore in nursery tales. Your *threads of thought* could lead you in lots of directions and, I'm sure, uncover many hidden memories and emotions.

For this chapter I follow the thread of *childhood things* and feature artists who explore dolls, fairy stories and imagined worlds in unique ways.

Personally, my love of old and used cloth pulls me back time and again to working with vintage baby clothing, especially if it's handmade. This tends to be simple in shape but with tiny stitching and often a decorative line of lace, which suggests to me a little bit of extra love being stitched in for good measure. These small items of clothing often provoke an immediate emotional response within the viewer, making them a powerful motif to use in your own stitched storytelling.

Nursery Threads of Thought

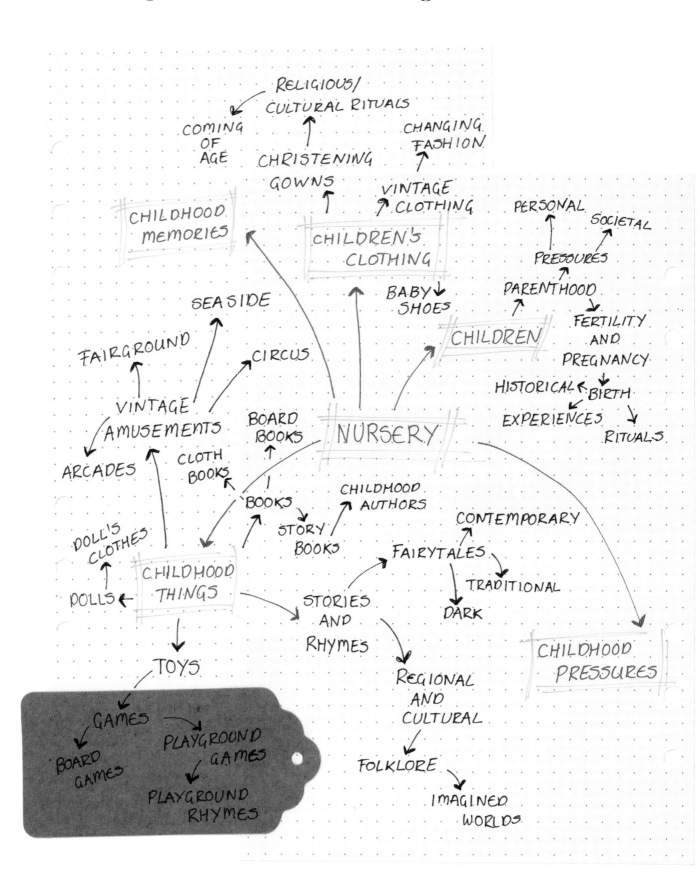

RELIGIOUS/ CULTURAL RITUALS

COMING OF AGE

CHANGING FASHION

CHRISTENING GOWNS

VINTAGE CLOTHING

PERSONAL

SOCIETAL

CHILDHOOD MEMORIES

CHILDREN'S CLOTHING

PRESSURES

SEASIDE

BABY SHOES

PARENTHOOD

FAIRGROUND

CIRCUS

CHILDREN

FERTILITY AND PREGNANCY

VINTAGE AMUSEMENTS

BOARD BOOKS

NURSERY

HISTORICAL EXPERIENCES

BIRTH

ARCADES

CLOTH BOOKS

RITUALS

DOLL'S CLOTHES

BOOKS

CHILDHOOD AUTHORS

CONTEMPORARY

DOLLS

CHILDHOOD THINGS

STORY BOOKS

FAIRYTALES

TRADITIONAL

DARK

TOYS

STORIES AND RHYMES

CHILDHOOD PRESSURES

GAMES

PLAYGROUND GAMES

REGIONAL AND CULTURAL

BOARD GAMES

PLAYGROUND RHYMES

FOLKLORE

IMAGINED WORLDS

Meaningful Materials

COTTON 'SUMMER DRESS' PRINTS

GINGHAM CHECKS

POLKA DOTS

SMALL CHECKS + STRIPES

OLD PATCHWORK QUILTS

CHILDREN'S HANKIES

CLOTHING:

        OLD PERSONAL ITEMS

        CHARITY SHOP FINDS

        VINTAGE CLOTHING

OLD NEEDLEWORK SAMPLERS

RIC RAC, DAISY TRIM, RIBBONS

PAPER FROM: COMICS

        STORY BOOKS

        SCHOOL JOTTERS

WORDS

CHILDHOOD MEMORIES

PARENTHOOD STORIES

CHILDREN'S FIRST WORDS

DATES + NAMES

STORIES FROM SCHOOL

        JOTTERS

CHILDREN'S WRITING ON:

        BIRTHDAY CARDS

        NOTES

        LETTERS

DIARIES + JOURNALS

RESEARCH DATA

Motifs

CHILDREN'S DRAWINGS & DOODLES

"CHILDLIKE" STITCHED DOODLES

STORY BOOK & NURSERY RHYME CHARACTERS

BOOKS, TOYS & GAMES

CHILDREN'S CLOTHING & SHOES

CREATING IMAGINED CHARACTERS

CREATING IMAGINED WORLDS

DOLLS   DOLL'S CLOTHES

TEXTILE BOOKS

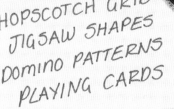

HOPSCOTCH GRID

JIGSAW SHAPES

Domino PATTERNS

PLAYING CARDS

Decorative story garments

Your nursery *threads of thought* will suggest ideas for motifs to use in your work. As a doting grandmother, I couldn't resist choosing a birthday card that was sent by my then four-year-old granddaughter Skye to her grandad. I'm not sure there's anything more exciting than watching a small child develop from making enthusiastically scribbled marks to creating identifiable, though anatomically suspect, drawings.

The beauty of using children's drawings as motifs is that they are often already in the form of simple lines that easily translate into appliqué and stitch.

For the following pages I worked with three vintage French baby vests. They were chosen for their simplicity of shape, each one enhanced by darns and signs of wear. You can find garments like these for sale online; I use eBay, Etsy and Instagram. I've listed some suppliers at the end of this book.

BELOW: *Love You*, 25 × 21cm (10 × 8¼in). Baby vest with simple Bondaweb appliqué and hand-stitching. Children's drawings can make beautifully personal motifs.

OPPOSITE: I traced my granddaughter's drawing and words onto vellum before tracing them onto the baby vest for stitching.

- You'll need a small garment (I only use natural fibres), scraps of cotton, a small piece of Bondaweb if you use the simple appliqué method, and threads. You'll also need a small embroidery hoop if working with a lightweight fabric.

- The shape of your garment will suggest the size, shape and placement of your motif.

- Draw your motif on tracing paper with a fine dark pen.

- The garment fabric will decide what method you use to transfer your motif onto your garment. I was able to trace my design through the lightweight cotton of my vest. I used a fine pencil line, but you could use water-soluble pen if you wish.

- If your garment fabric is thicker, use tissue paper and the method outlined in Chapter Two.

- Trace any areas to be appliquéd onto Bondaweb, reversing the image if needed, and iron onto your chosen fabric. Lightweight cotton is ideal.

- I stretched my vest in a hoop and stitched my drawn lines with backstitch, but use stitches that will best represent whatever motif you have chosen.

- Remove the hoop and iron on any appliquéd areas and add any extra stitching.

FURTHER DECORATION
- Using a limited palette of threads, I like to further decorate my garments by highlighting the lines of the garments themselves, around

necklines, hemlines and armholes. I add tiny patches in places and will often make a line of stitching around an old darn to draw attention to it.

THINGS TO CONSIDER
- Areas that are heavily stitched (such as the hair in my drawing) may distort a lightweight fabric. Build up the stitching a bit at a time, taking it out of the frame and pressing as you go along.

- If you're working on a lightweight cotton garment, the back of your stitching or threads may show through to the front, especially if you choose to hang your finished piece where light may shine through. I work on each area individually, starting and finishing my stitching by working the threads into the back, leaving a tail at the start of stitching and working it in at the end. For example, I stitched each eye individually rather than trailing the thread between them.

Baby list

I love how some things in life can be pretty mundane at the time but then in later years take on a huge significance because you know how the story plays out. My ex-husband recently found a little notebook that belonged to me filled with 'to do' lists from our early years of marriage. It was an everyday object back then but a treasure now.

Although many pages brought back memories, the one that I found particularly emotional was my baby list, where I had listed everything required before our first baby was born. Noted beside each item was where it would come from and how much it would cost. I was twenty-three and we were already hard up, so our budgets were planned down to the last penny. Anything that I could make, I did,

with blankets being refashioned from 'blankets at home'.

I photocopied my notebook pages, enlarging them slightly, and then planned the layout on tracing paper before tracing them onto the front of each vest with a sharp pencil. I used an embroidery hoop and stitched each word individually with backstitch.

Taking time over a project like this allows you to fully engage in the process. Not just the process of forming stitches but the process of remembering, the process of feeling and of becoming part of the memories once more.

Think about different ways that you could stitch personal words, even those that have no value to anyone else, as long as they touch you in some way.

OPPOSITE: *Baby Vest*, 53 × 23cm (21 × 9in). Vintage baby vest with hand-stitching. I enlarged the words from my original notebook before tracing them onto my vest and stitching.

OPPOSITE, BELOW: *Baby Vest, Cont.*, 50 × 20cm (19¾ × 8in). As well as stitching the words, I love to emphasize the shape and edgings of garments by adding decorative stitch.

LEFT: My baby list. These words immediately transport me back to that time of excitement and terror!

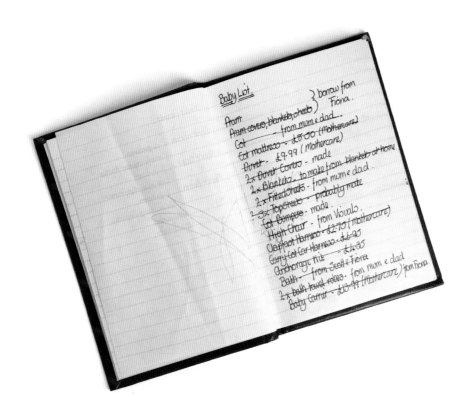

Baby List

Pram   } borrow from
Pram covers, blankets, sheets) Fiona
Cot   - from mum e dad
Cot mattress   £8·50 (Mothercare)
Duvet   £9·99 (Mothercare)
2 x Duvet Covers   made
2 x Blankets   to make from blankets at home
2 x Fitted Sheets   from mum e dad
3 x Top sheets   probably make
Cot Bumpers   made
High Chair   from Visuals
Claspfast Harness £2·75 (Mothercare)
Carry Cot Car Harness £6·95
Anchorage Kit   £4·35
Bath   from Scott e Fiona
2 x bath towel robes   from mum e dad
Baby Carrier   £3·99 (Mothercare) from Fiona

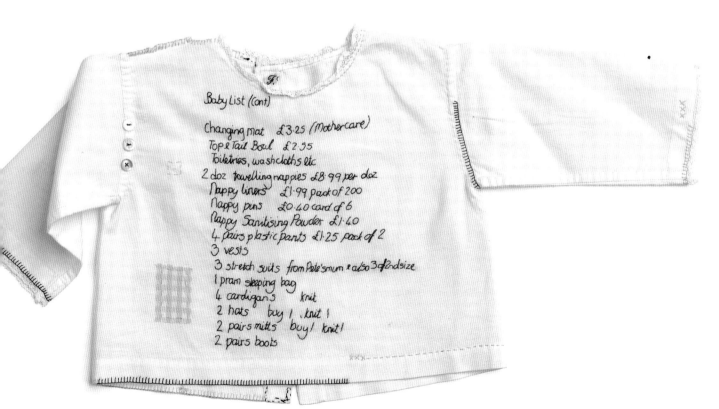

Baby List (cont)

Changing mat   £3·25 (Mothercare)
Top e Tail Bowl   £2·55
Toiletries, washcloths etc
2 doz towelling nappies £8·99 per doz
Nappy liners   £1·99 pack of 200
Nappy pins   £0·40 card of 6
Nappy Sanitising Powder £1·40
4 pairs plastic pants £1·25 pack of 2
3 vests
3 stretch suits from Pete's mum e also 3 of 2nd size
1 pram sleeping bag
4 cardigans   knit
2 hats   buy 1, knit 1
2 pairs mitts   buy 1 knit 1
2 pairs boots

ABOVE AND OPPOSITE, ABOVE: *A Place to Return.* Although these words are deeply personal to me, they can also connect to the viewer. The baby shoes make an instantly engaging motif.

LEFT: *A Shy Little Girl.* My childhood dancing shoes, tiny scraps of feed sack fabrics stitched in place with seed stitch. Words stitched on silk organza.

OPPOSITE: Small scraps of fabric are pinned onto the cotton batting ground to hold them in place for stitching.

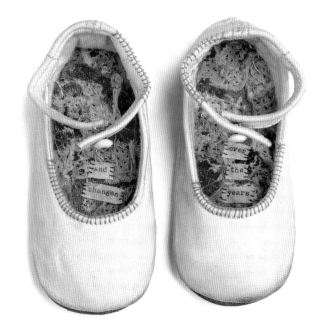

Baby shoes

This is another favourite motif of mine. I can't resist buying tiny leather baby shoes, the scruffier the better!

A Place to Return is made from a collection of leather baby shoes. The words come from my wedding vows: 'A place for family to return to as it grows and changes over the years'. My children were already young adults when Paul and I got married, so 'Home' took on a new meaning as we planned our future together.

I removed the insole of each shoe and used it as a pattern to cut a foundation

from cotton quilt batting. I covered this with the tiniest scraps of old fabrics and pinned these into place before stitching down with hundreds of seed stitches. The words are typed onto old cotton tape and stitched in place. I've highlighted the lines of the shoes themselves with small areas of stitching.

The words are small and unnoticeable unless you are up close, but it's the intention behind them that is important as they hang in the hallway of our home.

Kathleen Murphy

Artist and maker Kathleen Murphy is perhaps best known for her hand-stitched, three-dimensional, character-driven work. These colourful pieces, highly detailed with embroidery, are a portal to an imagined world – a vast wooded landscape called Skyruda Binrog. Verdant with over-sized leaves and vivid hues, this landscape is populated by tribes such as the shy woodland dwellers known as Silva Populi.

Inspired by fairy tales, folk mythology and a curiosity about what may lurk in the woods, Kathleen has always been a keen reader. After discovering an old mending kit as a child, she quickly discovered that she could use the needle and thread to draw and make in 3D the stories that swirled around her head. Her desire to tell stories through the medium of stitch continued into adulthood.

At the heart of her practice is her imaginative use of found or repurposed materials, making the most of the 'commonplace' household items that she finds or is given.

Kathleen explains: *'I've always loved the tiny details in illustrations or paintings, which you have to get in close to appreciate. Elements that give away more of a story than words alone. It's something I do in my own work, adding layers of stitched detail that might only be revealed if a mask is removed or a pocket looked into. I enjoy the challenge of getting these recycled or non-traditional materials to submit to the will of my needle. The scrap of tweed from a coat, a piece of discarded chopstick or a milk bottle top may not be obvious or evident when the piece is finished, but I take great satisfaction knowing that they are an integral part of the character providing form, stability or decoration. It's a pleasure to see an audience transported to another place created by using only humble, often overlooked materials and a simple sliver of metal and thread.'*

OPPOSITE: **Kathleen Murphy, *Ursino*, height 17cm (6¾in).** Scraps of vintage cloth, muslin, tweed, wool-mix felt, wire, wooden cotton reel and acorn cups. Stitched and embroidered by hand.

BELOW: **Kathleen Murphy, *Atticus*, figure height 17cm (6¾in).** Naturally dyed cotton, vintage napkins, felt, painted wooden spoon, vintage jar with wool tweed and natural moss. Embroidered and hand-stitched.

101

Caren Garfen

Meaningful materials, words and the use of powerful motifs are at the core of artist Caren Garfen's textile practice. She is known internationally for her challenging issue-based art.

Caren specializes in textiles, meticulous hand-stitching and intensive research. When these facets are combined, the artworks become discourses relating to issues that affect us as a society.

Caren says: *'The use of cloth, its tactility and familiarity within our lives, makes it the perfect tool for engagement. Textiles, text, the use of the tiniest of stitches and carefully chosen objects, draw in the viewer to reveal unexpected narratives.'*

Caren explains: *'Grimm's Fairy Tales were used as propaganda during the Third Reich. In 1940,* Little Red Riding Hood *(Rotkäppchen) was twisted into a tale of the wolf who was characterized as a big, bad Jewish character who devoured the innocent little German girl and her grandmother. Little Red Riding Hood skipped through the wood in a cloak decorated with swastikas and was rescued from the Big Bad Wolf by a man wearing an SS uniform in the guise of Adolf Hitler.'*

In *Babes in the Wood*, a vintage German fairy-tale puzzle has been carefully chosen to remind us that the twelve young children represented in this artwork did not live long enough to enjoy their toys.

Caren says: *'The puzzle has been adapted to tell the fate of these Jewish infants. Their short stories have been hand-stitched onto cloth and adhered to one facet of each block. On another facet is a photograph, digitally printed onto cloth, with each innocent soul holding their favourite toy, be it a doll, a teddy bear, or a bucket and spade. This artwork is in remembrance of the 1.5 million innocent babies and children who were murdered during World War II.'*

Caren Garfen,
Babes in the Wood,
15 × 15 × 26cm
(6 × 6 × 10¼in).
Vintage wooden Grimms' fairy tale puzzle, textile, silk threads. Hand stitch and digital fabric printing.

Mandy Pattullo

Artist Mandy Pattullo uses antique materials, often taken from unpicking old quilts, that hold a story of previous use. She allows the viewer to find a new beauty in her precious fragments.

Mandy's work often explores the relationships between cloth, family stories, objects and memory. In her collection of hand-stitched peg dolls, she reconnects with her childhood memory of Romany people coming to her grandmother's farmhouse door to sell clothes pegs. Romany folk used to carve these from willow collected from the Great Yarmouth marshes and then take them from door to door to sell for ready cash. Her grandmother always bought some pegs, in fear that she would be cursed if she didn't. These items, which have been made for centuries using nearby wood and bound with reclaimed tin, do indeed carry a hint of ancient magic.

Sometimes Mandy's grandmother would use the pegs to make simple dolls, and Mandy carries on this tradition. Dressed in reclaimed cloth, these dolls have a talismanic quality that celebrates Mandy's love of folk art, diversity (there are never two exactly the same) and female friendship, and showcase her unique collection of worn fabrics.

Mandy Pattullo, peg dolls. Hand-carved wooden pegs and hand-stitched cloth from Mandy's unique collection of worn antique textiles.

Unknown stories: taking inspiration from chance finds

This little tin came into my possession several years ago, and it fascinated me from the moment I opened it. It was full to the brim with snippets from newspaper and magazines, cut out roughly but carefully collected and kept.

I discovered that most of the cuttings were from the British magazine *Woman's Weekly* from during the long years of the Second World War. I know nothing about the owner, but I like to think that she drew comfort from her weekly ritual of collecting little snippets of hope and storing them safely at a time when optimism was in short supply.

Among the cuttings I found several titled 'Name This Child'. There was a different name each week, with an explanation of the meaning attributed to it. This caused me to wonder. Perhaps this lady suspected that she was pregnant and, with her husband or sweetheart absent, she collected names to ponder deliciously until her baby was born. But as I sorted, I discovered there were too many names to have been simply collected during pregnancy.

My imagination then conjured up a newlywed, her married life stretching in front of her but cruelly on hold, as she spent her evenings alone. Longing for a baby and the trappings of married life, she cut out each name and stored it safely for when normal life would resume once more.

Sometimes these very special finds come your way quite by chance. You feel goose bumps when you spot them and an unexplained emotion as you handle them. Sometimes you just know

that you want to use them in some way but have no idea how.

For me the key is to really notice the thoughts that come to mind as I handle these things and to pursue these thoughts. Finding out that many of the clippings were from wartime *Woman's Weekly* magazines prompted me to track down a few copies. Flicking through the pages, I found myself imagining someone else doing the same – every Tuesday, week in, week out. From there, my story started to take shape.

You'll probably never find the truth when working with these chance finds – and I wouldn't want to as that would feel intrusive – but the real story will be contained in your work anyway, hidden but woven in with your own imaginings.

My tin of cuttings led me to track down wartime *Woman's Weekly* magazines, offering a glimpse into domestic life at that time.

106 weeks of waiting

The title came about because I discovered there were 106 'Name This Child' snippets, cut and collected over 106 weeks. I wondered how I would while away my evenings, alone but longing to start a family, so I decided to create a small patchwork quilt using the cuttings.

I arranged my patchwork of cuttings onto iron-on interfacing and ironed them in place. Where possible I preserved the original cut edges. Being flat and firmly attached to the background helped protect the paper from tearing as I worked. I added the patches in stages and stitched as I went along, again to protect the paper.

My original plan was that the quilt would be the size of a small cot but left unfinished. However, while I was immersed in the making, I decided to fragment it, shattering the dream, so I cut it into three pieces.

I finished each piece with cotton quilt batting backed with cotton, the three layers knotted together as a tied quilt would be. I then trimmed all three layers and finished with a rather irregular buttonhole stitch.

I used 101 of the 106 cuttings to construct my quilt pieces, leaving five nestled with all the other snippets in the original tin. It felt important to leave a few in place to keep the real, hidden story intact.

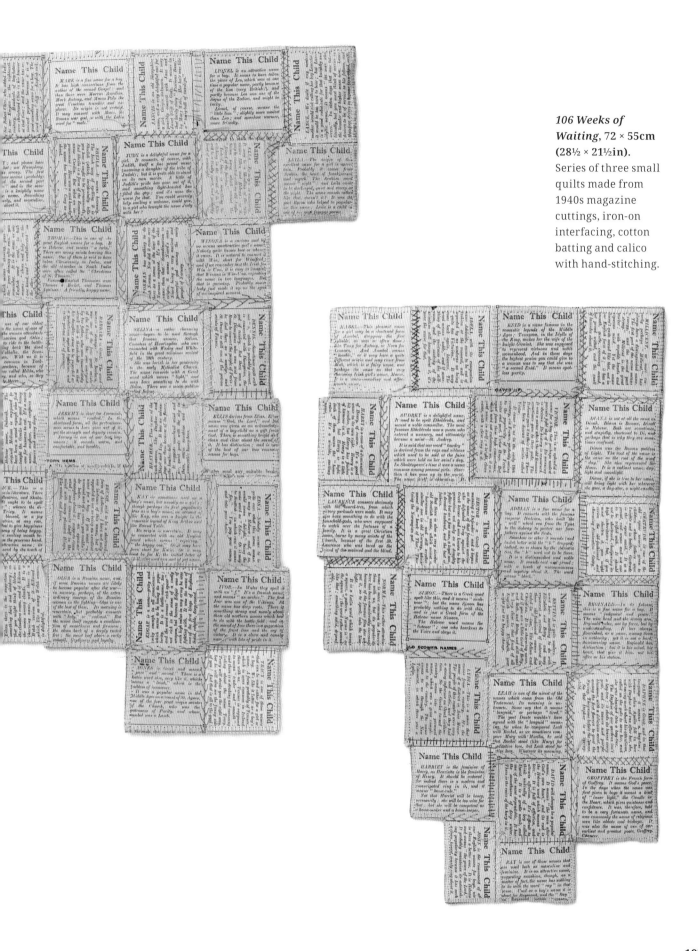

106 Weeks of Waiting, 72 × 55cm (28½ × 21½in). Series of three small quilts made from 1940s magazine cuttings, iron-on interfacing, cotton batting and calico with hand-stitching.

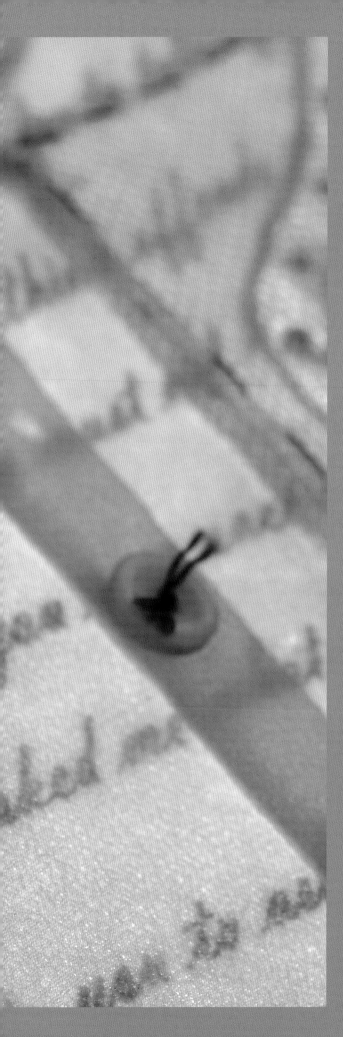

Bedroom
Stories

I'm sure your bedroom *threads of thought* will lead you in many potential directions, but I found that my own explorations took me to the private and personal. I think of exploring personal stories, whether my own, researched or imagined.

My thoughts take me immediately to the wardrobe and to clothing, the inspiration for many of my textile pieces. While the wardrobe houses our outer layers of dress, the underwear drawer represents, in my mind, our secrets and vulnerabilities. Not only the actual things that we hide away because they are precious or private but also the personal, vulnerable parts of ourselves that we hide carefully from others.

You could also explore the dressing table and mirrors with thoughts of how we see ourselves, of body image, of beauty and of ageing. And, of course, while exploring the bedroom, we can't forget the bed and its many associations.

Let's start our bedroom explorations by looking at items of clothing as motifs for storytelling.

Bedroom Threads of Thought

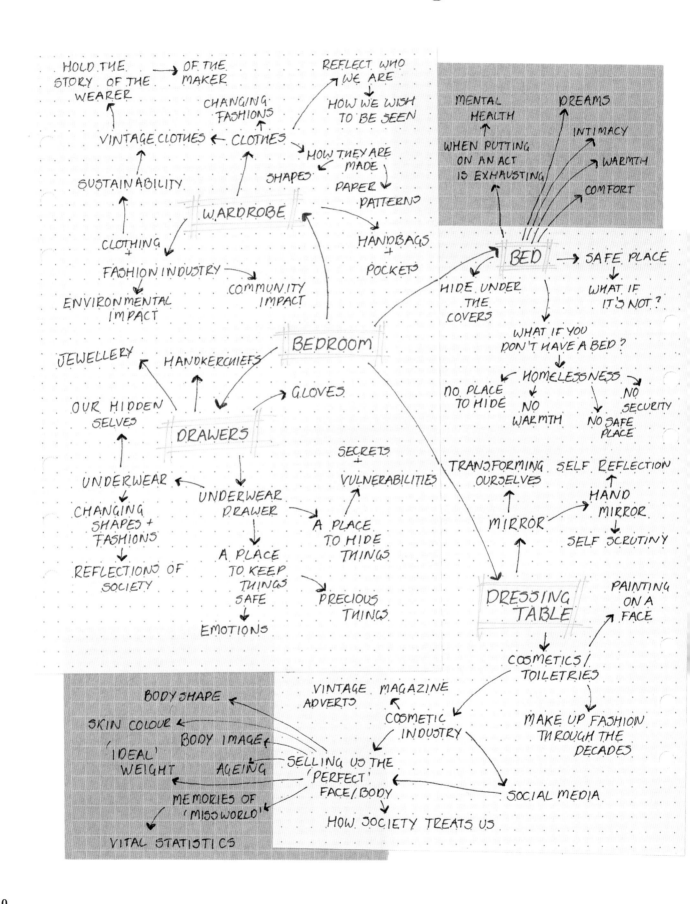

HOLD THE STORY OF THE WEARER → OF THE MAKER

CHANGING FASHIONS

REFLECT WHO WE ARE

HOW WE WISH TO BE SEEN

VINTAGE CLOTHES ← CLOTHES

HOW THEY ARE MADE

SHAPES

PAPER PATTERNS

SUSTAINABILITY

WARDROBE

HANDBAGS + POCKETS

CLOTHING + FASHION INDUSTRY

COMMUNITY IMPACT

ENVIRONMENTAL IMPACT

BEDROOM

MENTAL HEALTH

WHEN PUTTING ON AN ACT IS EXHAUSTING

DREAMS

INTIMACY

WARMTH

COMFORT

BED → SAFE PLACE

HIDE UNDER THE COVERS

WHAT IF IT'S NOT?

WHAT IF YOU DON'T HAVE A BED?

HOMELESSNESS

NO PLACE TO HIDE

NO WARMTH

NO SAFE PLACE

NO SECURITY

JEWELLERY

HANDKERCHIEFS

GLOVES

OUR HIDDEN SELVES

DRAWERS

SECRETS + VULNERABILITIES

TRANSFORMING OURSELVES

SELF REFLECTION

HAND MIRROR

MIRROR

SELF SCRUTINY

UNDERWEAR

CHANGING SHAPES + FASHIONS

UNDERWEAR DRAWER

A PLACE TO HIDE THINGS

REFLECTIONS OF SOCIETY

A PLACE TO KEEP THINGS SAFE

PRECIOUS THINGS

EMOTIONS

DRESSING TABLE

PAINTING ON A FACE

COSMETICS / TOILETRIES

MAKE UP FASHION THROUGH THE DECADES

BODY SHAPE

SKIN COLOUR

BODY IMAGE

'IDEAL' WEIGHT

AGEING

MEMORIES OF 'MISS WORLD'

VITAL STATISTICS

VINTAGE MAGAZINE ADVERTS

COSMETIC INDUSTRY

SELLING US THE 'PERFECT' FACE / BODY

HOW SOCIETY TREATS US

SOCIAL MEDIA

Meaningful Materials

SENSUOUS FABRICS:
- SILK + SILK ORGANZA
- LACE
- FINE COTTON LAWN

CLOTHING:
- OLD PERSONAL ITEMS
- SECONDHAND FINDS
- VINTAGE GARMENTS

GARMENT PIECES:
- OLD DETACHABLE COLLARS
- LACE COLLARS
- MODESTY PANELS

VINTAGE SHEETS + PILLOWCASES

BLANKETS, PATCHWORK QUILTS + EIDERDOWNS

OLD HANDKERCHIEFS

EMBROIDERED DRESSING TABLE SETS

PAPERS:
- COSMETIC PACKAGING
- ADVERTS FROM OLD MAGAZINES
- TISSUE PAPER + TISSUTEX

PERSONAL EXPERIENCES

LOVE LETTERS

MARRIAGE, BIRTH + DIVORCE CERTIFICATES

FACTS + FIGURES FROM THE FASHION INDUSTRY

FASHION MAGAZINES

WOMENS / MENS MAGAZINES

WORDS ABOUT BODY IMAGE

COSMETIC ADVERTISEMENTS

VINTAGE BOOKS + MAGAZINES

FAD DIETS

MENTAL HEALTH EXPERIENCES + DATA

✕ Motifs ✕

VINTAGE HATS, GLOVES, HANDBAGS & SHOES
COMPACTS & LIPSTICKS
GARMENT SHAPES
CORSETS, GIRDLES & SUSPENDERS
HAND MIRRORS
VANITY SETS
WEIGHING SCALES
TAPE MEASURES

Cheryl Kennedy

Assemblage artist Cheryl Kennedy creates beautifully sculpted dresses honouring the strong women that were part of her rich heritage. Her use of materials transforms the merely decorative into powerful domestic icons.

Cheryl is based in the rural town of Castlemaine, Central Victoria, Australia. The local countryside provides a rich source of found objects, which, together with her collection of textiles and memorabilia, enable her sculptures to tell a story. Her extensive library of materials is the starting point for all her work.

Cheryl transforms the unexpected mediums of metal and wire into soft flowing movements that could not be achieved by using fabric alone. She strips back the layers of the old and the discarded and rebuilds them into a new narrative; a new story. The adornments on the dresses represent an insight into the personality and story of the wearer.

Cheryl explains: 'Laura *is named after my husband Leo's maiden great-cousin, whose relatives travelled the world before the First World War.'* The metal baggage tag references their travels.

OPPOSITE: Cheryl Kennedy, *Mathilde,* **60 × 60cm (24 × 24in).** Wire and fragments of an old French quilt. The soft materials make a beautiful contrast to the metal.

BELOW: Cheryl Kennedy, *Laura,* **60 × 60cm (24 × 24in).** Wire and pressed metal with metal luggage tag. The tag is a wonderful motif for telling stories of travel.

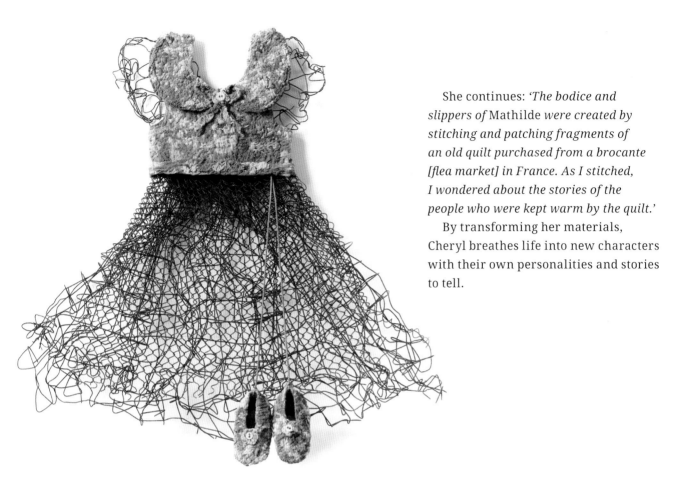

She continues: *'The bodice and slippers of* Mathilde *were created by stitching and patching fragments of an old quilt purchased from a brocante [flea market] in France. As I stitched, I wondered about the stories of the people who were kept warm by the quilt.'*

By transforming her materials, Cheryl breathes life into new characters with their own personalities and stories to tell.

Deconstructed story garments

While Cheryl *constructs* her garments from metal, wire and her imagination, I *deconstruct* old garments and use their shapes as motifs to illustrate people and tell their stories. I use the combination of old and worn garments with words and handwriting taken from found correspondence to create imagined stories from the lives of complete strangers.

There's something really satisfying about the process of deconstructing a piece of clothing. I start by carefully inspecting it, noticing the shapes and construction of necklines, armholes, pockets, collars and cuffs. I'll look

for button bands and buttonholes, removing plastic buttons and replacing them with linen or mother of pearl. I notice signs of wear and tear and look for darns or mends – for me the most precious part of the garment!

I then start taking it apart through a combination of unpicking seams, cutting and ripping, making the most of interesting shapes as they emerge. Taking apart old garments can reveal beautifully shaped interlinings in collars, cuffs and sometimes yokes.

I collect all of these pieces together and they become my materials to rearrange and piece together to create a new story.

The underwear drawer: secrets and vulnerabilities

'I just wish each and every hour away, and yet still they drag.'

I was captivated the first time I read these words and became smitten with the author Peggy and her husband Jimmy. The words are lifted from a collection of six intimate letters sent between the couple during the last three years of the Second World War. This was a much treasured chance find from eBay.

I know very little about this young husband and wife except that they were both based in wartime Britain but separated by circumstance. I only have tiny glimpses into their story; the rest is purely in my imagination.

Sketchbook page, 44 × 30cm (17½ × 12in). My sketchbook page showing repetitive writing of one of the phrases that captivated me from Peggy and Jimmy's love letters.

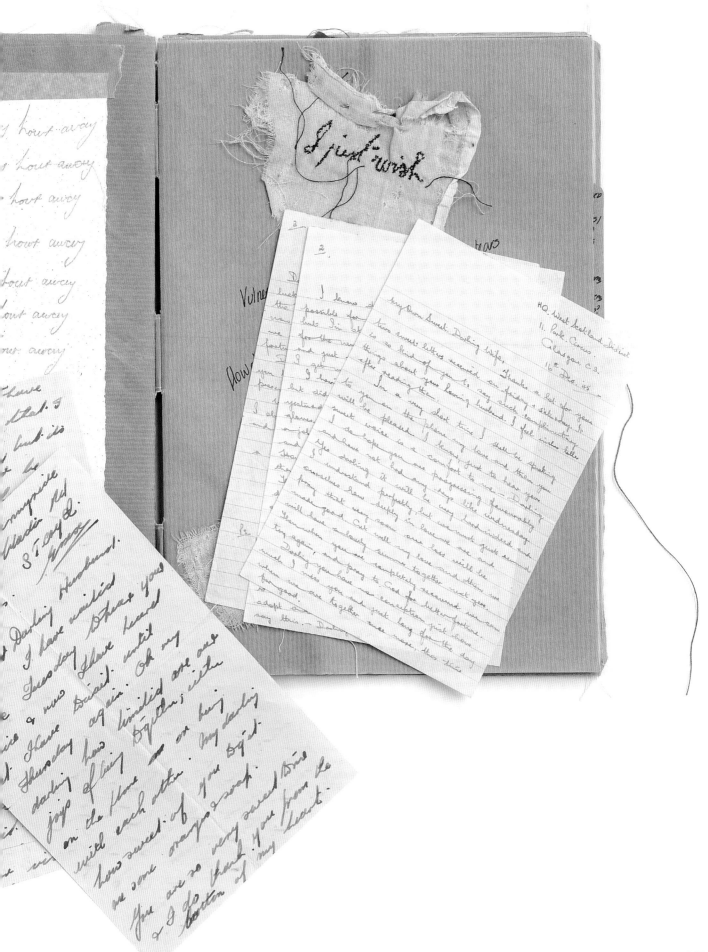

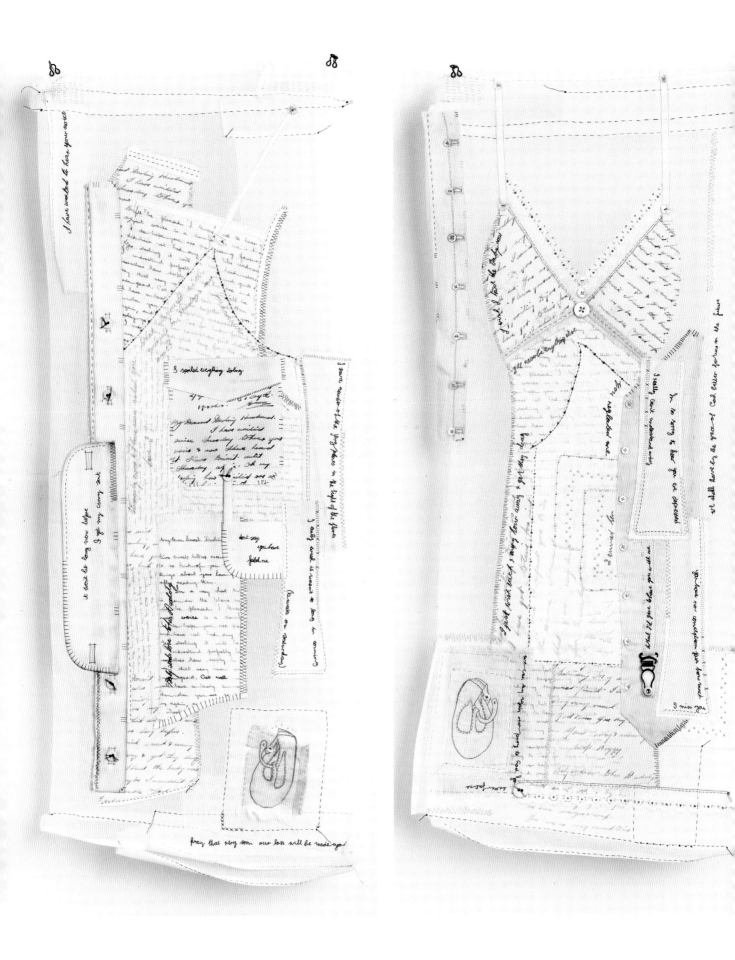

Baby sends love

I created my story of Peggy and Jimmy using meaningful materials, words and motifs and, broadly speaking, the making process outlined in Chapter Three. I read their letters many times over, jotting down the phrases that particularly spoke to me at each reading. I rewrote certain phrases over and over, copying each stroke of the authors' handwriting until they became so familiar I could've written them blindfold.

The first three letters written in 1942 are bold and flirtatious, but the other three are different. Dated from 1945, they are emotional and melancholic. V. E. Day has come and gone, and Jimmy is still waiting to wear his 'civvy suit'. Peggy sounds depressed and vulnerable but she's also pregnant, signing off 'baby sends love to daddy'. Sadly, three months later Jimmy sends a heart-breaking letter of love and support and 'prays to God for better fortune'. This set the narrative for my story.

I started with Jimmy's story, gathering together garments to illustrate it. I chose a white shirt, because his words are stoic, strong and positive. I used the interlining from a shirt collar, the part of the collar that is hidden away, as a suggestion that maybe everything isn't as it appears on the outside. Of course, Peggy's story is inextricably linked with his, so I included a piece of a vintage camisole to layer in among his things.

I used coffee to lightly stain some of the fabrics and cut everything out to make the most of the garment shapes. The materials are layered onto a silk organza background as I wanted a delicacy to the piece as a whole.

The words are from both Peggy and Jimmy, from conversations that go back and forth. Pages from the letters are inkjet-printed onto cotton, silk organza and Tissutex paper (see next page for process) and applied with Bondaweb, acrylic medium and stitch. Motifs abound with the shape of each piece of clothing and the blue baby shoe in the corner, stitched in vintage blue silk.

I created the outline of a full-length slip as my main motif for Peggy's story, taking apart an original 1940s slip to use as the pattern. Peggy's words expressed her emotional turmoil, so I turned to the underwear drawer for her clothing inspiration, using the other half of the vintage camisole, part of a modesty panel, and an old handkerchief from my mother-in-law's hankie drawer. I used the outer layer of Jimmy's collar – the brave face he was wearing for her.

I also added pieces of vintage lace and snippets of an old silk petticoat, reusing its seams and stitching lines. I wanted to include a bit of the flirtatious Peggy from the earlier years so included a suspender or garter clip with the words 'what I'd give to have you with me' stitched in silk.

I layered the silk organza background in places, strips and patches creating interesting lines of stitching with words hiding between layers. I repeatedly used the selvedge of the organza and rather love the way it curls in places.

These two pieces are inspired by emotion rather than fact, so they hang suspended in space, wafting gently with the movement around them. It saddens me that such personal words have ended up in the hands of a stranger, but I like to think that perhaps I have captured some of their spirit and that by spending many hours stitching their words I'm honouring their real story in some very small way.

OPPOSITE, LEFT:
Baby Sends Love – Jimmy, 35 × 92cm (13¾ × 36¼in). Silk organza, deconstructed garment pieces, with inkjet-printed text and hand-stitching. Words from Peggy and Jimmy's letters.

OPPOSITE, RIGHT:
Baby Sends Love – Peggy, 37 × 87cm (14½ × 34¼in). Silk organza, deconstructed garment pieces, vintage buttons and suspender clip with inkjet-printed text and hand-stitching. Words from Peggy and Jimmy's letters.

Adding written stories with Tissutex

I add text to garment pieces by inkjet-printing it onto 9gsm Tissutex paper (similar to the paper tea bags are made from), then bonding this onto fabric.

To print

- Test print your text on ordinary printer paper.

- Cut your Tissutex slightly larger than a sheet of printer paper.

- With a glue stick, run a line of glue along the top and bottom edges of a piece of printer paper and carefully attach the Tissutex, smoothing it as you go.

- Leave to dry, then carefully trim the excess Tissutex.

- Place in your printer feed tray to ensure that it will print onto the Tissutex side. I use standard print settings.

- After printing, remove the backing paper and leave to dry thoroughly.

- Iron your print.

To apply to fabric

- I use an acrylic matte medium (Liquitex) to paste my Tissutex sheet onto my fabric, but you could use watered-down PVA.

- Spread your acrylic medium evenly over your fabric, covering the entire surface. Remove excess medium with your brush.

- Carefully apply your printed Tissutex face up. Smooth it down with a clean, dry brush or a rag as you go. Remember your print may smudge if you get it wet. If there are any air bubbles, gently peel back your sheet and apply more acrylic medium and smooth down once more. Leave to dry.

If you are applying words to a garment shape, trace the outline onto your Tissutex after it has been printed and cut to shape. Carefully apply as above.

BELOW: Sample showing Tissutex that has been inkjet-printed and then cut out and applied to this bodice shape.

OPPOSITE: *My Dear Child*, 18 × 30cm (7 × 12in). Deconstructed child's bodice with words taken from a mother's letters. The letters were inkjet-printed onto Tissutex and applied as before.

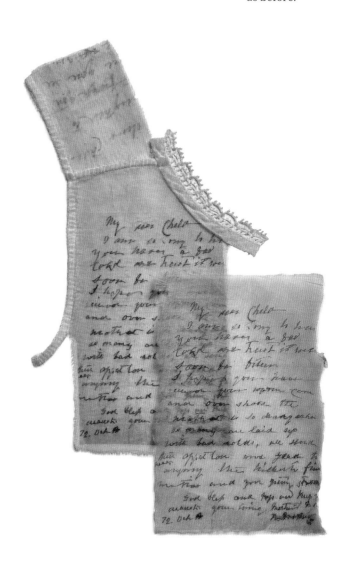

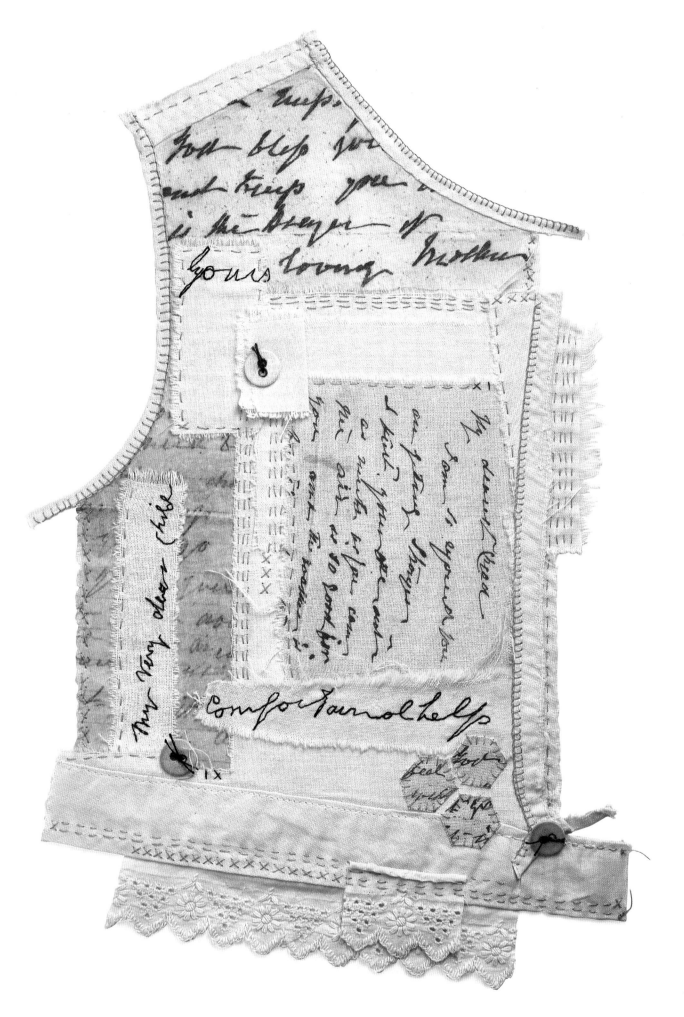

Hidden selves: Not just blue

Not Just Blue, 48 × 75cm (19 × 29½in). Deconstructed baby dress, cotton lawn, silk scraps with the hand-stitched words of mothers describing their experiences of postnatal depression.

This piece was inspired by a creative art project that I delivered many years ago with different groups of parents within family support centres in my community in Midlothian, Scotland.

During the first session I asked if anyone would like to discuss anything. One woman said she wanted to talk about postnatal depression. She shared her experiences, then one of the most emotional discussions that I have been involved in began as, one by one, women across all the centres opened up and told their stories, several for the first time.

We wrote everything down, direct quotes of the women's words. We went on to create a quilt made from paper patches held together with tape, staples and safety pins, a different voice in each patch. Titled *Barely Holding it Together*, this quilt was displayed in health centres across the community.

I returned to my notes again years later, deciding to bring the women's words out in the open once more.

I gathered my materials: a vintage baby dress, the hem and seams of a silk petticoat, and a background of very fine cotton muslin. I hand-dyed the dress blue without using a fixing agent and immediately rinsed it to remove most of the colour. The chosen materials and placement of pieces result in a finished piece that is scrappy and fragile. The words are hand-stitched in backstitch, an investment of my time in words that were unspoken for a long time.

These stories still go untold: behind closed doors, women still feel isolated, ashamed and that they are the only ones feeling this way. I imagine the pressure to be 'happy' and seen to be 'coping' must be even higher in these days of social media.

My hope is that this piece opens up conversations showing others that they are not alone and perhaps giving them courage to speak out and ask for help.

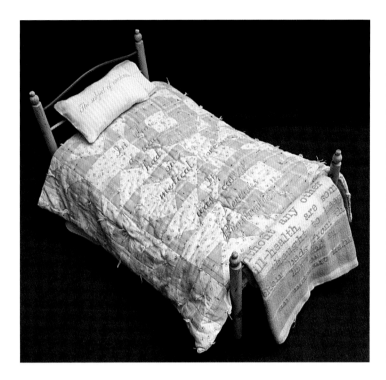

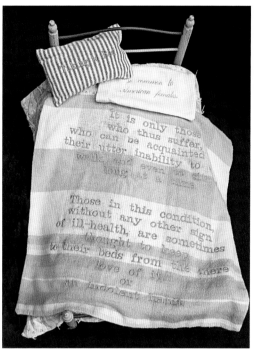

Tamar Stone

Artist Tamar Stone's work is inspired by her interest in women's lives in the nineteenth and early twentieth centuries and the constrictions placed upon them by clothing and societal expectations. This, combined with her interest in the history of housework, has led her to tell wonderfully intimate 'women's stories' through her creation of unique 'story books' made from dolls' beds and antique salesmen's sample beds.

Tamar's beds feature words that are stitched onto every surface – both sides of quilts, pillows, pillowcases, layers of blankets, sheets and even on the front, back and sides of mattresses.

As Tamar explains: *'in order to read these intimate stories the reader must unmake each bed, pulling back the covers to "turn the pages". In order to close the work (book), one must re-make the bed, mimicking the actions of women's housework that have been done for centuries.'*

Taking to Bed tells of women whose stories of sickness revolve around 'taking to bed'. Tamar says, *'I think of being wrapped up in bed coverings with the women in this piece and hearing about their struggles. In some ways I find it comforting.'*

The words tell of women's experiences of depression in the 1860s, quoting the personal experiences of American writer Charlotte Perkins Gilman and including words from author Mrs L. G. Abell, whose advice of 'getting up and moving around would be good for a person' (stitched on the back of the quilt) seems to be very forward-thinking for the time.

They are machine-stitched onto old household materials such as an antique quilt piece, vintage cotton sackcloth and a piece of vintage cotton plaid blanket – fabrics that have themselves had a past life in someone's most personal space.

ABOVE: **Tamar Stone,** *Taking to Bed*, **30 × 53 × 33cm (12 × 21 × 13in).** Antique wooden doll's bed, antique quilt front hand-tied with backing of cotton sackcloth, vintage cotton blanket with machine-embroidered text.

Vulnerabilities: love tokens

Like everyone else, my world turned upside down in 2020 when the global pandemic hit and we went into lockdown. As uncertainty grew, I found it daunting to work outside in my studio on some of my larger projects, so I retreated indoors and started working small.

I gathered together a collection of my favourite cloth scraps, mostly from a piece of 1940s feed sack quilt that was so worn that it tore into fragments in my fingers. I stashed these, along with a selection of vintage silk threads, into a little 'mobile studio' in the form of an old three-compartment loaf tin.

I was drawn once more to Peggy and Jimmy's love letters and found that many of their words and phrases resonated with the thoughts and emotions now tumbling around within me. Each time a phrase from a letter jumped out at me, I'd trace it onto vellum and add it to my tin of gatherings.

I spent hours stitching their words onto leftover pieces of silk organza and my tiny scraps of homely fabrics. Picking them up and setting them down just as the mood took me, it became a project that didn't require thinking, just steady stitching.

Creating these tokens became a soothing activity, comforting and healing as my heart ached from missing my special people. Each one is decorated with tiny stitches. I renamed seed stitch 'worry stitch' during lockdown!

These pieces are worn, torn and look a bit battered (weren't we all) and somehow all the more special for that.

Only fabrics that were comforting and brought joy made it into my mobile loaf tin studio!

A project like this is ideal for when your hands and heart need to stitch but your mind is elsewhere.

- Gather together a collection of fabric scraps and threads. You'll also need a fabric to use as your foundation. I used an old quilt backing that ripped easily because I wanted the tokens to be textural and scrappy. Gather scraps of transparent fabric for your writing and trace or write your words onto them in pencil. I used silk organza.

- Store all of your gatherings in something that makes rummaging easy. You'll also need a small embroidery hoop. I used a 15cm (6in) one. Stretch your foundation fabric over your hoop, then layer and pin fabric scraps on top. I use entomology pins as they are long and very fine. Pin your fabric with pencilled words on top.

- Make your thread selection. I used vintage silk thread, but a single strand of embroidery cotton is perfect. I started by sewing my words, worked in a tiny backstitch on the organza. I then stitched down the scraps using simple stitches – running, blanket and hundreds and hundreds of tiny seed stitches.

- When you are finished, either rip or cut your background, keeping in mind that unless your fabric is very worn it will only tear along the straight grain. If you keep your stitches away from the very edge of your cloth scraps, you can use tiny scissors to cut away the background fabric, leaving your token with gorgeous scrappy edges.

Love Tokens,
**Average size
7 × 10cm
(2¾ × 4 in).**
Scraps from
1940s quilt and
silk organza on
foundation of an old
quilt backing.

Conclusion

I do hope that in reading my thoughts and stories, your own have started to emerge and that you are inspired to explore them with *threads of thought*, personal materials, words and motifs. This simple process can, of course, be used to explore any subject or theme, so the possibilities are endless.

You may have noticed that I repeatedly use snippets of the same fabric and keep returning to the same sources for words and motifs. This is because these things continue to speak to me, and it would feel somewhat rude to discard them mid-conversation! The personal *threads of thought* that I created during the writing of this book will provide me with inspiration for years. I'm excited to play around with the many ideas that have come to me while writing, and I have been diligent with my thought catching and have scraps of paper with scribbled notes carefully stashed away for the future.

I've presented the projects as suggestions for ways of working rather than step-by-step instructions; they're deliberately inspirational rather than prescriptive. I urge you to experiment and follow your own paths.

Let go of the idea of creating finished pieces if you can, and approach projects with the attitude of trying things out. By continually asking the question 'How could I...?' you'll find a way of working that is personal, meaningful and authentic. The finished pieces will emerge in their own time.

I hope you enjoy your explorations!

No Need to Languish, 26 × 37cm (10¼ × 14½in). New fabric prints sit beautifully with old feed sack cottons, table linens, a dressmaking pattern and items of vintage haberdashery.

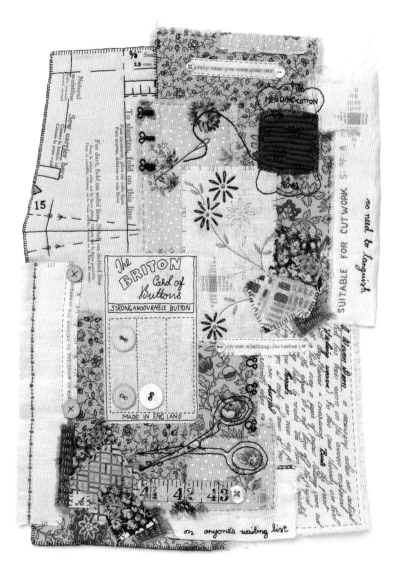

Dear Nora, 25 × 35cm (10 × 13¾in). Cloth collage using vintage and feed sack cottons, table linen edging, paper recipes, inkjet-printed calico and vintage buttons with hand-stitching.

POST CARD

Dear Nora
Hope the weather
keeping from ...
... are ...
... the time ...
... will arrive ...

Harold

You are invited...

Miss N. ...
... Scarborough

Ginger and Lemon Cakes

½ lb. creamed butter.
½ lb. soft brown sugar.
cupful golden syrup.
cupful treacle.
1 level teaspoonful bicarbonate soda.
½ cupful milk.
lb. sifted plain flour.
1 teaspoonful ground ginger.
½ teaspoonful mixed spice.

Grease a shallow baking tin, 13 inches b...
...nes. Beat butter and sugar to a cream. ...
syrup, treacle, and soda dissolved in ...
...k. Sift flour with ginger and spice. Stir...
...ter mixture. Pour into prepared tin. Sp...
...ch corner with a palette knife.
... on the middle shelf of a fairly slow o...
...F., Regulo 2 to 3) till risen, firm ...
browned) in about ...

"**What wonderful tea,**" said Jim's mother
(—and gran' I glad I kept a special caddy of Brooke Bond 'Choicest'!)
I'd spent days cleaning the house before Jim's mother
came to stay for the first time. She was very sweet—and
quite surprised to see how well looked-after her darling boy
was! But it wasn't until tea time that she really relaxed.
"What wonderful tea," she said. "It must make a big hole in
your housekeeping to get tea like this."
"Oh no," I said, "it's Brooke Bond 'Choicest' and it's not at
all dear or difficult to get. I always keep a special caddy
for occasions like this."
"Mmm," she smiled. "That's a habit I'll start when I get hom...
a fragrant blend of choice Ceylon an...
...t it is undoubtedly the best value in
...ddy of Brooke Bond 'Choic'st' for

Bro...
A ...
...te

Drink Me

Tea Cake. H...

Rub 1 oz butter into ½ lt
of self raising flour, salt ¼,
dessertspn sugar mix well.
Beat an egg, add to it
2 tablespns milk stir all in
Bake ... well gre...
tin in ... Cut
in she...
hot

Suppliers

GEORGE WEIL
for Freezer Paper, Bubble Jet Set 2000,
Tissutex
www.georgeweil.com

DEBORAH GREENSILL
for French garments and cloth
instagram.com/dsg1964

WENDY SHAW
for vintage cloth and paper ephemera
instagram.com/ticking_stripes

A VINTAGE AFFAIR
for vintage domestic treasures
instagram.com/a.vintage.affair

DONNA FLOWER
for vintage cloth and quilt pieces
donnaflowervintage.com

VINTAGE BUTTON EMPORIUM
for vintage and antique buttons
www.vintagebuttonemporium.com

Contributing Artists

Caren Garfen	www.carengarfen.com
Tina Gilmore	Instagram.com/partofyourstory
Cheryl Kennedy	Instagram.com/cherylpkennedy25
Vanessa Marr	www.marrvanessa.wordpress.com
	www.domesticdusters.wordpress.com
Kathleen Murphy	www.theowltheharethehuman.blogspot.com
Mandy Pattullo	www.mandypattullo.co.uk
Tamar Stone	www.tamarstoneart.com
Maria Thomas	www.mariathomastextiles.co.uk
Haf Weighton	Instagram.com/hafweightonartist

Acknowledgements

My heartfelt thanks to the following:

The wonderful team at Batsford, especially Nicola Newman for her expertise and support.

Michael Wicks for his fabulous photography.

The contributing artists for sharing their own cloth stories.

Amgueddfa Cymru – Museum Wales for permission to include images of 'Feast'.

Inspirational tutor Kim Gunn for re-introducing me to mind maps and thus starting this thread of thought …

My family, including my four gorgeous granddaughters who will go on to tell our family's stories in their own unique ways.

To Paul who shares all my stories – both the exciting and the mundane.

And to my mum – who can make, stitch or fix absolutely anything!

All photography by Michael Wicks except for the following:

Gavin Crumpton page 77

Paul Ferguson pages 6, 26, 29, 30, 32, 44–45, 46, 47, 51, 61, 79, 84, 95, 96, 99, 118, 119, 122 and 123

Caren Garfen pages 23 and 102

Ian Hill page 113

Julie Hough page 112

Rhian Israel pages 52–53

Vanessa Marr pages 23 and 64

Kathleen Murphy pages 100 and 101

Mandy Pattullo pages 104 and 126

Tamar Stone page 121

Maria Thomas pages 50 and 65

OPPOSITE: **Mandy Pattullo, peg dolls.** Hand-carved wooden pegs and hand-stitched cloth from Mandy's unique collection of worn antique textiles.

RIGHT: **Collars.** I use vintage detachable collars as a strong motif in telling men's stories. Here with paper, fabric scraps, machine and hand-stitching.

Index